MARRIED
TO THE DEVIL

MARRIED TO THE DEVIL

True Life Story

AMANDA TWEED

authorHOUSE®

AuthorHouse™
1663 Liberty Drive
Bloomington, IN 47403
www.authorhouse.com
Phone: 1-800-839-8640

© 2012 by Amanda Tweed. All rights reserved.

No part of this book may be reproduced, stored in a retrieval system, or transmitted by any means without the written permission of the author.

All the names in this true story have been changed, apart from those of the author, Amanda Tweed; the co-author, Mrs Yvonne Jarvis; the pastor at LOMI Birmingham, David Jarvis; and the apostle at LOMI International, Dr. Steven Richards, who is the general overseer.

Published by AuthorHouse   07/24/2012

ISBN: 978-1-4772-1442-8 (sc)
ISBN: 978-1-4772-1443-5 (e)

Any people depicted in stock imagery provided by Thinkstock are models, and such images are being used for illustrative purposes only.
Certain stock imagery © Thinkstock.

Because of the dynamic nature of the Internet, any web addresses or links contained in this book may have changed since publication and may no longer be valid. The views expressed in this work are solely those of the author and do not necessarily reflect the views of the publisher, and the publisher hereby disclaims any responsibility for them.

Contents

Acknowledgements ix

Chapter 1   My Childhood 1
Chapter 2   Being a Green Teen 8
Chapter 3   First Encounter with the Law 15
Chapter 4   The Prince of Darkness 21
Chapter 5   The Day I Took Control 31
Chapter 6   Returning Home to Birmingham 39
Chapter 7   The Hand of God 58
Chapter 8   Divorcing the Devil 73
Chapter 9   What Drugs Can Do to a Soul 82
Chapter 10 Finding Jesus Christ 87
Chapter 11 The Big Fall from God 93
Chapter 12 Reunited with Jesus Christ 106

A Final Word 115

What others are saying about Amanda Tweed and the book *Married to the Devil:*

A lot of Amanda's experiences I can feel and also relate to. I didn't know Amanda when she walked in the dark places, but seeing her now I find it really hard to believe that this woman led such a life. After reading this book, I broke down in tears. This book is a real page turner, and I've been left wanting more. A miracle has happened.

—Cheryl Louise Humphries

Laughter, tears, and happiness are some of the emotions I recall with this young lady. I can relate to Amanda's dark places. Although our paths didn't meet, we certainly travelled down the same road. What a powerful and a very inspiring testimony.

—Lisa Juliet Foad

Astonished . . . Wow. I didn't really believe in God before meeting Amanda and sitting down to read her true-to-life book. I now believe in something. If it works for Amanda, then why not for me?

—Karl Day

I met Amanda in Brooke House. During a conversation with her, she openly told me about some of her past. I was shocked even to think that this woman had led such a dark and terrible life. A few weeks after meeting Amanda, I sat with her and some of the other residents in the house, and we watched a DVD of Amanda at a family gathering filmed in 1992. After watching the DVD, Amanda showed me a photo of her on a prison ID card from when she was in HMP Brockhill in 2004. I was completely lost for words. Comparing the photo to her current appearance, I could see that a big transformation has taken place in this woman's life. I could clearly see that in the photo taken in 2004 her candle was not burning and her soul was lost.

—Anthony Richards

Amanda has come a long way. She certainly was saved from the dark world of drugs and crime so that she can fulfil the purpose for her existence. Amanda is now the light of the world. She will be sent back to people who are like she used to be to deliver them from the forces of darkness that are leading them to destruction. Amanda is now working with the Greater Light, God, the Creator of the heavens and the earth. Souls will be saved. Thank you, Lord Jesus.

—Pastor David Jarvis

I am humbled by Amanda's salvation and her new life.

—Mrs Yvonne Jarvis

All the names in this true story have been changed, apart from those of the author, Amanda Tweed; the co-author, Mrs Yvonne Jarvis; the pastor at LOMI Birmingham, David Jarvis; and the apostle at LOMI International, Dr. Steven Richards, who is the general overseer.

Acknowledgements

THANKS TO MY spiritual mom, Mrs Jarvis. Without your support I wouldn't have had the ability to write this story. God told me that you are a gift from Him to me. You've fed me spiritually, and your obedience to God is something to be adored. I'm also aware that you are diligently seeking the Lord on a regular and daily basis as you pray earnestly from your heart. You have been there for me when I've had super tantrums and didn't rise to me, and that is a gift of longsuffering, a lot of love, and the patience of a true saint. You are always willing to share the love of Jesus, and your teachings on abiding with Christ are conveyed with the love of Jesus. You gave me the opportunity to be rehabilitated back into society when society recognised me as just a name and number, and that is no recognition. God bless you, lady. Thanks also to my pastor, David Jarvis. Your obedience to God where your sheep are concerned is to be admired as you teach us how to keep our eyes on the Lord. I and others recognise the way that God is using you mightily; praise God. I thank God for your life, sir. Thanks as well to Apostle Stephen Richards. Your teachings are very powerful, and what I saw in you the day I met you drew me closer to my Lord and Saviour, and for that reason, I appreciate your life and thank God Almighty for blessing me with your life. Thanks are also due to a very special aunt who never once turned her back on me even when I was at my lowest. You know who you are, my love. You always had faith that one day I'd be free from spiritual shackles and bondage. I also know that you sought the Lord and prayed earnestly from your heart for my life, and at last your prayer has been answered—glory to God. Thanks to a very dear friend of mine—you know who you are, chick. You supported me through thick and thin and never turned your back on me. In fact, you invited me in, fed me, loved me, and always had a kind word from the heart for me. You supported me when I was imprisoned, and on my son's birthday, you gave him a gift and told him it was from me, because that's the sort of person you are. God bless you, my love. Lenni you've been a big inspiration too, sweetheart. You have kept me going, making me laugh from the pit of my stomach even on days when I didn't think I had a laugh in me. You also gave me a chance when no one else dared to have that faith in me. Thanks, little sis. I have faith and know that the God of our Lord Jesus Christ will bless you too, so you had better make room to receive your blessings. Amen. Thanks to Lisa Lou, who was also with me as I wrote this book and was my backbone when I wanted to throw in the towel. You too are a strong testimony that God is a true and faithful God as He works wonders in your life. Mommy, you laid your hands on me and prayed to the Lord that day I was released. I thank the God of our Lord Jesus Christ for your life, and I thank Him for your obedience; you are a gift from the most-high God. He used you mightily to pray for me that day as I walked out of HMP Drakehall. Thanks to the single ladies who I met on my last prison tour at Drakehall from November 2010 to January 2011. To each and every one of you who supported me and were true mates, I have not forgotten you, and we will be reunited one day away from prison walls. May God keep you all safe until we are together again in body and spirit. I've left the best until last. I am eternally grateful to the Holy Spirit, who led me in a way I never would have believed possible. Father, you brought all these wonderful people into my life, and without the Spirit of the sovereign Lord, none of this would have been possible. I thank you, Father, for giving me all the wonderful things in life. I thank you for blessing me with all these wonderful people that are all in my life for a purpose, and I believe by faith that the purpose is to fulfil Your word. I thank you for saving me and loving me because you are the living God whose word is true and never returns void. I thank you for everything that seemed impossible. You make all things possible in Jesus Christ's mighty name. Amen.

Chapter One

MY CHILDHOOD

I WAS BORN in November of 1968 on my granddad's birthday. It was quite ironic, really, since he loved a drink, and when he was drunk he used to always say to my mom, "Christine, when are you going to have the baby?"

Christine and James Tweed are my beloved parents whom I put to the ultimate test, and I've really tested their faith in God Almighty. I took them to hell and back!

I was the second of seven children. I've got three brothers and three sisters.

When I was two-and-a-half years old, my parents, my elder brother, my younger brother (who was born in February of 1971), and I moved to an area called Nechells from our previous home in an area called Smallheath, both in the city of Birmingham.

In 1973, Mom gave birth to twins, a boy and a girl, so there were seven of us living in a small, three-bedroom flat. Most week-ends I spent visiting my grandparents, who lived in an area called Edgbaston also in the city of Birmingham. As a child, I was very happy and contented and much loved too. I was surrounded by big love from my family. I felt that I was very lucky, as my aunts and uncles from my father's side of the family were like my big brothers and sisters. As I was the second eldest, I usually felt like the big sister to all my siblings, so it was nice to be the baby amongst my aunts, uncles, and grandparents.

Because my granddad and I shared a birthday, we would spend our special day together. My granddad would make me a cake, and I'd have a card, money, and a box of Milk Tray chocolates. Also, one of my aunts is only eighteen months older than me, and we were best friends. We were never separated. I recall making popcorn with her, and my nan, whom I called Mommy, didn't mind us experimenting with flour and water to make dough. I was very close to my grandparents, aunts, and uncles. I was also very close to my Dad. I can recall him taking me out with him to buy me a pair of shoes. He took me into an expensive shoe shop and told me to try on a pair of shoes. They were sensible shoes and were brown (Dad's favourite colour); they were the most comfortable shoes I had ever worn, but because they were brown and plain, I played up in the shop, saying the shoes were pinching my feet and rubbing at my heel. Dad asked one of the assistants to measure my feet. Once my feet were measured, my dad and the assistant said they couldn't understand why the shoes were causing me discomfort, but I think my dad knew that I was playing up and that I didn't like the shoes. I learned that Dad wasn't backing down to my play acting, and he decided that he was going to buy me the shoes anyway. He also saw that I liked a pair of blue sandals and got them for me as well. He also brought me a swing for our garden. Although Dad got the swing for me, he made sure that I shared it with my younger siblings. I travelled a lot with my Dad. He plays the steel pan and was in a group, and sometimes I travelled with him to different venues. I loved soca music, and I wasn't shy to get down low on the dance floor. I had a very close bond with my dad. My mom had to juggle caring for us, cooking, being there when we were ill, and loving us all. I used to underestimate the power of my mom's love. My mom never stopped. She hand-washed our clothes when she couldn't afford to go to the launderette, and going to the launderette was a treat, I can tell you! Although I wasn't as close to Mom as I was to Dad, she's my Mom and she did her best to bring us up; it really wasn't easy for her. We always had the best clean clothes, and we got what we asked for at Christmas. I think the reason I wasn't as close to Mom was that I spent a lot of time around my grandparents, aunts, and uncles on Dad's side of the family. I called my nan Mommy, or if I was talking about her to someone I referred to her as Granny Tweed. I was well loved; it hurts so much. I never really knew my mom's mom. I knew who she was, but I never knew her. Yes, she was my nan, but I don't have many childhood memories of visiting her. I also recall two of Mom's sisters visiting us when we lived in Nechells. I suppose it was because I was always at Mommy and Papa's that I didn't see much of my mom at week-ends, and she worked very hard to make our flat a home for us all.

The local primary school was down the road from where we lived on Cromwell Street and was therefore called Cromwell Junior and Infant School. I went there from age five to eleven. I have quite a few good memories of that school from the whacky teachers to my school mates. I recall sports day one year when I lost the running race and came second. I was gutted, as I'd always come first in the past. Christmas parties were something to look forward to; the teachers made an effort at Cromwell school. We also had penny discos on Friday afternoons! We'd pay our 1p and boogie the afternoon away. Those were the days. I also recall the tuck shop and the bottles of milk with the skinny blue straws. That was a regular and normal thing back in the Seventies. I also joined the school choir, and I remember our music teacher, as he was quite strict. At Christmas, before the end of school term, we'd have festive plays and perform with singing and play acting for the local OAPs and our relatives. I remember all our plays were based on the birth of Jesus Christ, Mary, and Joseph—oh, and the three wise men. Although my grandmother (my mom's mom) was a Christian woman who went to the local Methodist church and my Mom had a little black leather Bible at home, I didn't know anything about this Jesus whom I saw my fellow schoolmates acting every year. In fact, I can remember trying to read the Bible when I was young. It was in our bedroom, and I remember picking it up one night. I started to read from the beginning in the book of Genesis. I read how God created the heavens and the earth and man and woman in six days and rested on the seventh day. I found the rest confusing and quite boring, so I put it down and never picked it up again!

I also recall one Christmas when the snow was virtually up to my waist (this was in the 1970s), as I wasn't very tall. In fact, *short* and *fat* were my mom's words to describe me. So there we were—Mom, my nan (my mom's mom), and me, walking in the deep snow going to my Nan's church, Saltly Methodist Church, about two miles from where we lived in Nechells. I recall the vicar talking, and I was so bored I really just wanted to go to sleep, but instead I sat and endured what seemed like a lifetime with some old man with a dog collar on going on and on about God.

My trials with church didn't stop there. No, my nan had the bright idea that me and my mom should come to church more often. I can recall going to Sunday school a couple of times, and I hated every minute of it. All these other kids were there, and they were right goody-two-shoes in the class, but I really didn't want to be here. I knew

God created the earth and that there was a place in the sky called heaven and a place below the earth called hell. I also knew it had taken God six days to create the world and that He had rested on the seventh day. I'd also heard about Adam and Eve; what more did I really need to know? When the Sunday school teacher was drooling on about Jesus, the Lord, and God, I was completely lost! I turned my little brain off, as I just wasn't interested. But the funny thing was that every night I'd pray before I went off to sleep. My younger siblings and I shared a room, and we'd all say a little prayer that our mom had taught us: "In my little bed I lie; Heavenly Father, hear my cry. If I should die before I wake, I give the Lord my soul to take. Amen." Then I'd say my good nights to my brothers and sister, to my parents, my grandparents, aunts, and uncles, and then to God, the Lord, Jesus, and the Holy Ghost. I was confused, because I'd heard God called by all these different names, and I said them all just so I didn't miss any out.

On 21 December 1980, my mom gave birth to another family addition, a beautiful baby girl. There was a twelve-year gap between the baby and me, so I naturally took on the role of the big sis and became a mother figure too. It was fun having a baby in the family after so long. She really was a beautiful child. I recall watching her sleep and leaning into her cot to kiss her chubby cheeks. I woke her up deliberately a couple of times just so I could cradle her and sing songs to her. Two years later, on 30 September 1982, another beautiful baby girl joined the Tweed family, and the role of big sis and little mom took me by force. The baby was also a beautiful child. She looked a lot like Mom, and her skin was so soft. I was an expert nappy changer. I made up the baby bottles, rocked the babies to sleep, told them bedtime stories, and so on. I really enjoyed being like a mom to my little sisters. Mom often went to designer stores and bought them pretty dresses, and they dressed identically too.

After the birth of the baby, we moved to an area called Stechford, as the three-bedroom flat was too small by far to contain our family. We moved to a five-bedroom house in a strange area. I continued to go to Duddeston Manor Secondary School in Nechells, as I'd already got settled in and my mom said that I should continue to attend that school, as I'd chosen my options for my exams. Besides, I'd already made my mind up that I wasn't wearing the local school's horrible bottle-green uniform.

Every morning, my younger brother and I caught the 14 bus to Nechells to go to school. I often smoked a cigarette upstairs on the bus, as it was allowed in the early 1980s. I sometimes saw a girl that also went to Duddeston Manor get on the bus about six or seven stops after me. She was bullied at school, because she wasn't very clean and was often called fat and ugly. Jennifer always looked sad and troubled, and although my mates didn't bother with her, there was no reason why I should follow suit. Whenever I saw her on the bus we would share a cigarette and talk about school. She wouldn't speak to me when she saw me in school with my mates, but I always said hello to her. I did feel sorry for her, but she had this I-don't-want-to-speak-to-anyone attitude about her.

My best mate at school was a girl named Jackie. We knew each other from nursery school, but I used to be so horrible to her at nursery that she begged her mom not to send her to the same junior and infant school as me. She often told me this, and I don't know how many times I told her I was sorry, as I didn't know any better at the age of three or four. We became really good mates, and in our maths class we really buzzed off our maths teacher, who wore the same blue suit every day. He was a bona fide alcoholic. He'd swear at us if he was in a bad mood. He stank of tobacco and booze and had yellow teeth. If he was in a bad mood and you answered the questions to your work correctly, he would put crosses next to your answers. However, if he was in a good mood, he'd give you ticks and write "bloody marvellous" in big red letters on your page. Even if your answers were incorrect, he would still tick the work and give you a big smile! I recall being in his class one day, and it was about fifteen minutes to the end of school. The fire alarm was ringing, and he ran and locked the classroom door with all of us inside. When someone shouted, "Sir, it's a fire drill and we have to evacuate the premises," he told that person to shut up, as he believed it was not a fire bell but the end-of-school, but no one was leaving until he was satisfied that we knew what he had taught us that day!

I also recall a time when I was in my computer studies class and the teacher had really bad breath. His Birmingham accent was very similar to that of Benny, one of the characters in the TV series *Crossroads*. Mr Parker sat at his desk while we were supposed to be working on our computers. My mate Monica and I had a devilish thought at the same time. She sneaked over to this lad and picked up his berry style cap. I cut the berry off the cap. We couldn't stop laughing. After a little while, we noticed that he was looking for his cap. I decided to stick his berry back on the cap using thick brown tape (the kind of tape used for parcels), and we set it down where it wouldn't be obvious we were the ones who had taken it. When he found his berry cap and saw that the berry had been cut off and stuck back on with brown tape, he went ballistic. To this day I don't believe we ever owned up!

Chapter Two

BEING A GREEN TEEN

As time passed, I became every parent's nightmare. I went out clubbing every week-end to the clubs and wine bars in the city centre. I remember Christmas Eve just a few weeks after we moved to Stechford. As I still went to Nechells every weekday to attend school, my schoolmates were everything to me, and our reputation wasn't hidden. We were loud and always played practical jokes on other pupils in our school. None of us really had any time for boyfriends; we thrived on girl power. I was thirteen years old, and I went to a blues party with a mate who was a year younger than me. When it was over, it was early hours on Christmas Day, and everyone knows that there isn't any public transport Christmas Day whatsoever. So I ended up staying over at my mate's, because I was tired and had no means of transportation. I woke up late in the afternoon on Christmas Day and had to brave facing my parents and the long, cold lonely walk from Nechells to Stechford, as I didn't know any short cuts. I got home in the early evening. I didn't know what all the fuss and upset was about. My parents and my siblings were distraught; the turkey hadn't met the oven. My parents looked as if they'd been on a crash diet, and all eyes were on me as if they'd just seen a ghost! My dad never used to smack us as kids; that was Mom's job, but on this day he made an exception. In the past, he had only to give us that look—you know the one where the eyes would do the shouting? Yeah, that one, but that day I felt my Christmas present! The way I screamed the house down, I'm surprised our neighbours didn't dial 999 for the police. I'm sure everyone who heard me really thought I was going to die from the way I carried on! But saying all that, I was a real drama queen with a capital Q. That was just one incident I was involved in as a young and green teen.

I used to meet up with my mates every Saturday and become a pain in the backside to the security guards in town. I never went out of my way to do anything, but we'd all meet up by the fountain, and the guards would continually ask us to move on. We'd walk away from the fountain, and then we'd return after a short while. I saw a few people get thrown in the fountain too! I stole make-up and fashion jewellery, as did most of my mates, but I never got caught. If my dad had found out, he would have hit the roof. My mom knew and told me to stop time and time again, but I was very disobedient and unruly. I was cheeky to my mom and answered her back. How she kept her hands from grasping me around my throat I'll never know.

I did do OK at school, passing exams in English, Mathematics, Biology, and PE. In 1983, I left school at the age of sixteen and went on a Youth Training Scheme. I worked in retail selling High Street fashion clothes, and on Saturdays the manager allowed me to wear the latest fashions to promote the garments. A couple of the girls that worked there didn't like the fact that I was allowed that privilege and were quite bitchy about it, and the fact is that the manager did pamper me a lot.

It was easy to rub other staff the wrong way, and it worked every time. I left that placement and worked in a shoe shop, but after a few weeks I couldn't stand the smell of sweaty feet all day long, so I left. However, I did end up getting another job working in another shoe shop which was very up-market! (The feet didn't really affect me that much there.) Two girls that I really got on with worked there too, and we went to the pub after work and sometimes on week-ends.

It was 1985 and I was sixteen or seventeen years old when I had the weirdest dream ever. I don't recall how the dream started, but the next bit I remember as if it was yesterday. I was walking on a golden beach looking at the calm sea which was the most beautiful blue I've ever seen. The sky was just as beautiful, as was the bright sun. I was with a stranger. I can't explain the colour of his skin. It's not that I don't recall the colour; I just can't explain the colour. I also can't explain what he looked like, as those two things have been removed from my memory, but I do know he was a picture of perfection. We were walking on the beach, and we talked. Here's the mysterious bit: when he spoke to me, a foreign language came out of his mouth, a language I'd never heard before in my life, but I understood every word. What was even weirder was when I talked to him, the same foreign language came flowing out of my mouth, but I knew what I was saying. One thing I will say is that it was the most peaceful dream I have ever had in my life. To my understanding, I opened my mouth to speak English, and this new language emerged from my mouth, but I knew what I'd said back to him. It was such a calm, tranquil dream, and I was so at peace. At no point was I afraid, and when I woke up I was extremely happy inside but had no idea why! I mentioned the vision to a couple of people to hear what they thought, as it was a really mysterious dream, but no one could tell me what it meant. I don't know why, but I thought it was God. When I mentioned it to a family friend who is religious (Seventh

Day Adventist), she told me it wasn't God because no one has seen Him. I also mentioned it to a mate who'd recently converted to Islam, and he said the same—that it wasn't God, as no one has ever seen God. So who was this man in my dream, the perfect stranger? I just thought I'd share that dream with you, as it has always been in the mists of my mind. I also had a vision one day whilst I sat in a maths class. I was kind of day-dreaming to begin with, and then I had a vision of the sun beating down on the earth, the sky bright and blue, and then there was a crack of thunder and the sky turned pitch black. I mentioned this to a few people, and one person told me that what I had seen was an eclipse. It was *not* an eclipse that I saw. The sky didn't just darken; it was as if it was midday one minute and then midnight the next. I saw a lot of strange things growing up.

Also when I was seventeen years old, I met a girl who became my best mate. She lived just over the road from our house. She and her mom and siblings had recently moved into the area from a place called Tamworth. My mate was a competitive disco dancer. She entered dance competitions all over the country and had joined a local dance studio in the area. One Saturday morning, she asked me to meet her at the dance studio she'd recently joined. She had stayed over at her nan's house in an area called Shard End just outside of Stechford, where we lived. She arranged to meet with me at the studio, so I made my way there to meet with her. I waited until the class had finished, but she didn't show up. I struck up a conversation with one of the teachers at the studio who taught ballroom dancing, and out of the blue he asked if I wanted a job in the studio. He knew I wasn't a disco dancer, as I'd explained this to him during our conversation about why I was there. So when he asked if I wanted a job, I initially thought it was a cleaning job or helping out in the café. When he offered me the job as teaching dancing I didn't really understand what he was saying to me.

I explained that this was the first time I'd ever been in a dance studio as I wasn't into disco dancing and never really had any knowledge of what it was all about. He said that my mate was going to be working on a Youth Training Scheme from Monday morning and there was room for me to learn what the position entailed. In the meantime, he wanted me to start as soon as possible. I agreed without really knowing what I was agreeing to. He then took me into a smaller studio and said that I could start by taking a private lesson with one of the pupils who was also a competitive dancer. Basically, I was thrown in the deep end and didn't really have a clue, but I got on with it. In the next six months, I was trained up to conduct my own keep-fit class, and as the current world champion disco dancers had joined the studio to teach, I learned from them. I took intense dance lessons to learn the moves and how to teach them. After I'd been teaching dance for a while, I got a job with a lot more responsibilities and a much healthier income in a place called Dudley in the West Midlands. After a short time in the dance studio in Dudley, I took my official exam to be a semi-pro teacher, and six months after that I took my final exam and became a qualified professional dance instructor. I also went to competitions with my dancers and judged at some of the venues.

Most week-ends I would go out clubbing with my mates. As time went by, I became close to another girl who was two years younger than me named Laura. We became really good friends. Every Saturday night, we went to a club called Tabasco's which was in an area called Witton in Birmingham not far from the city centre. We had some laughs in that club. We had a deal. If I met a bloke, she had to make an effort with his mate and vice versa. I'm sure she used to look for a good looking guy with a not-so-good-looking mate so that she could have a laugh at my expense! I know the thought of doing that to her crossed my mind a few times! We used to have a lot of laughs. We were very loyal to one another when we were out clubbing. We went out together and went home together no matter what happened.

In March 1988 my granddad was diagnosed with cancer. Although I worked in Dudley and passed Dudley Road Hospital on my way to work, I never once visited him when he was there. The last time I saw my granddad was in a pub called the White Swan on Victoria Road, Aston. He was telling someone that I was his first granddaughter. I remember thinking he'd got it wrong and saying to him, "I'm your second grandchild," as I've got an older brother. But he corrected me and said, "No, you're my first granddaughter. My first grandchild is your brother." He was admitted to hospital shortly after I saw him in the pub. A few weeks later, my mom received a phone call from the hospital letting her know that her dad had passed away. That was the first death in the family, and it was my granddad, Mr H. His birthday was May 1, and he died a couple of days before that. A short while after he died, I dreamed that God asked me what I wanted. I just remember a voice in the sky. I said, "Lord, my granddad has died, and I never saw him before he went. Can I see him, please?" I recall seeing a beautiful blue sky with the sound of birds singing sweetly, and there he was, my granddad, smiling just like he used to when telling someone that I was his first granddaughter. He was smiling down from the clouds at me. He looked really happy. All of a sudden, there was a loud crack of thunder and it went pitch black and I saw him no more. I thanked God for showing me my late granddad.

After that dream, I found peace in my life concerning the loss of granddad. The guilt I felt before having that dream was unbearable. I knew there was a God and I believed that He was from above. I just didn't understand anything about Him. My mom told us as children about judgement day, and I used to visualize the whole world standing before God and Him asking us questions like, "Why did you do this wrong and that wrong whilst you were on earth?" It was too scary to think about as a child, so I tried not to think too much about judgement day. Now let's move on.

I started dating a guy called Simon. Because I was a dance instructor, I never wanted any children, as I wasn't parental and wanted to keep my flat tummy and all my curves. Although I enjoyed playing mom to my younger sisters, I liked the fact that I could hand them back to my mom when the going got tough.

In April 1989, I found I was pregnant. When I was only a few weeks into the pregnancy, I didn't want Simon anywhere near me! I don't know what it was, but I didn't like him very much when I was pregnant. Not very nice, I know, but hey, that's hormones for you!

Chapter Three

FIRST ENCOUNTER WITH THE LAW

On 3 February 1990, I gave birth to a beautiful baby boy. I found being a new mom quite exciting and really enjoyable. I christened Josh when he was five months old. I tried to get a hall booked for 29 July that year, as that's my older brother's birthday and I felt it would be nice to have a double celebration. However, that date was unavailable, so I opted for the week before. My grandparents loved him dearly, as he was the first great-grandson, and he was a comical baby. He never really cried, but when he did, he sounded like a little lamb. Josh was seventeen months old when Papa died of a blood clot in his brain from bumping his head on the fire-place in my grandparents' home while he was drunk one night. I was absolutely devastated, as it was a sudden death. I was visited by a wild bird, which I believed was a sign of death. Let me explain. I went to a keep-fit class at our local community centre. I arrived at the community centre half an hour early. I was familiar with the care-taker, as I had held keep-fit classes there in the past, so I was trusted to unlock the studio. It was when I let myself into the studio that I came face-to-face with a sparrow flying around the room. I panicked, because my mom had once told me that it was a sign of a death when a wild bird entered a room. I had a gut feeling that someone close to me was going to die, but I didn't know who. So when later that night my mom's house phone rang and my mommy said she thought Papa had died, I instantly knew he was already dead. I was heartbroken. He was buried exactly a year to the date after Josh's christening, 22 July 1992. Josh was too young to know what had happened, but I knew I'd be spending every birthday in the future differently.

Josh was a good baby until he hit age two! I continued to teach, and on most occasions I took my son with me to the dance classes, and what a challenge that was! But it was worth it, as he was a happy and contented child. I only taught dancing part-time after school hours. My clients included all ages, from children to adults, so I also worked part-time jobs in the mornings and early afternoons. From 1992 to 1995, I worked in a well-known betting shop as an assistant manager and watched as the punters threw their money down the drain. Don't get me wrong; I saw a few people win, but I also saw a hell of a lot more lose! Later on in 1995, I decided to work in our local post office. I enjoyed working as a post-office cashier, and the transactions were quite interesting.

Because I started my new job very near to Christmas that year, I hardly had any money. Looking back, it really didn't matter, because we all had a nice time and no one went without a huge dinner and presents. But when I was approached by someone to commit fraud, it didn't take too much persuading, especially considering the money that was involved. I started off with small amounts; £6,000.00 was my first hit. Then it quickly escalated to £10,000 and £15,000.00. After a few weeks, I was taking £45,000.00 on an average day. Some days I'd take about £20,000.00 in the morning and then another £40,000.00 in the afternoon. This went on for six months. The post-office staff didn't have a clue. It was Tony (the man I was dating at the time) who led the police to me through his stupidity. He was bragging in a casino one night, and the staff contacted the police. He was also heavily involved in the scam. All my friends and family thought that I'd bagged myself a wealthy man because of the amount of cash I had in my possession. I didn't tell anyone what I was doing, but I couldn't look Granny Tweed in the eye, as I felt guilt grip me. The amount of money I took out of the post office was scandalous. If you think six figures, then you'll have an idea! It all came to an end on 16 December 1996. I was arrested and charged with conspiracy to steal. Then, after I appeared in court, the charge was dropped to theft from employer. I had several court appearances from December 1996 through May 1997. It was May 1997 when I received an eighteen-month custodial sentence and was sent to HMP Brockhill, Redditch. However, it was my first time to be in front of the courts, and I didn't have a previous criminal record. I also had a very good solicitor. As a result, out of the eighteen months, I had to serve nine. One of the things a lot of haters couldn't accept was the fact that the police and courts didn't confiscate a penny from me even though they had seen documentation and goods that I had acquired with the stolen cash. The police had seen all of my household items, clothes, car, and jewellery, as well as the cash receipts to prove I'd been a very busy lady indeed, but they left me with all the possessions I had acquired through my criminal activities! I admitted the offence in police interview, as I was caught bang to rights. The judge told me that he had respect for me, as the police raid had recovered a Christmas list which showed that I was planning to spend a lot of the money on my immediate family. All the clothes I owned were designer clothes. I kid you not when I say that with the amount of clothes and cosmetics I owned, I could have easily opened a pretty huge shop!

I started my sentence in a closed prison, HMP Brockhill, Redditch. I recall walking through the prison gates in handcuffs escorted by a Group 4 officer from Birmingham Crown Court. I arrived in the reception area, where I was asked a series of questions regarding my next of kin, home address, and so forth, as well as a lot of security questions. I was also strip-searched, as this procedure is a must for everyone who walks through the prison gates from court. The officers were quite friendly as they introduced themselves and explained prison life to me. I wasn't that scared, actually. I think it was the initial shock before I was sentenced. This was my new home for nine months, and I could either allow it to break me and consequently spend the time the hard way or get on with it knowing that I was not going anywhere and I had to make the best out of a bad situation. After the reception department, I was led to the induction wing, which was D wing, and was put in a dormitory with three other inmates. As soon as I walked in, I saw the faces of three ordinary women who, like me, had broken the law. I immediately warmed to them and they to me. One of the women in the cell was pregnant and was talking of having a visit with someone who she hoped would bring her drugs. I used to judge people for being careless with their children, but look what I had done, and I had no excuse apart from the love of money. Greed is a terrible thing. We had a toilet in our cell, and we ate our meals around a dinning table situated by the staff office. I was only on D wing for a couple of days, as I was considered a prisoner who could look after herself by the officers and my fellow inmates. Some women are extremely vulnerable in prison and very timid. I had always been able to look after myself, and I never looked at prison as a place where I felt threatened. I was moved to C wing on the main side of the prison, where I was put in a cell. In my cell was a single bed nailed to the hard, cold floor; a mini-wardrobe with a chest of drawers attached; and a metal desk where I sat to eat my meals and write my letters to my people in the outside world. There was a toilet in the recess area, as we didn't have toilets in the cells on the main side. I made it my home, as it was where I had to lay my head. I met a lot of women there to whom I got quite close. As I was a female DJ and wrote all my own lyrics, I used to entertain some of the girls during association time. Most of the women I spoke to in prison were addicted to heroin or crack or both. That was the first time I ever saw heroin in my life. There was no way I was going down that road; I didn't really understand what made people want to destroy themselves and wasn't shy in voicing my opinion. Based on the memories I hold of that prison sentence, I'm quite confident that I can write a book on what it's really like behind prison walls. I remember being in my cell after lunch when an officer unlocked my door and told me to pack my things, as I was to be shipped out to an open prison. I didn't want to leave the girls I'd met, as we had become really close. There were tears and broken hearts as we said our good-byes. I wasn't alone on the ship-out; there were another five or six girls going to HMP Drakehall with me.

We arrived at the open prison, and it was very different from a closed jail. It looked like a little village. There was a farm on the prison grounds where some of the inmates had been given the job of looking after chickens. Once we settled in and were shown our rooms—not cells—it not only looked like a village but was like living in one too. Some of the other women serving prison sentences didn't look like your average criminals, if you get my drift, and others you could tell had been in and out of prison for years. As time went by, I found myself adapting to prison life, as this open jail held no real punishment. Yes I had been sent to prison, locked away from the outside world, friends, and family, but once I had served two-thirds of my sentence, I was eligible for town visits and home leave. My family visited me every single week without fail until I was allowed to visit them. My dad would then drive down to the prison to pick me up in the morning, and I had to be back by a certain time. I remember coming back from one town visit in particular. I was on time (according to my watch); however, my personal officer was working in the reception department. Not only was I late, but I'd had a drink and was slightly tipsy too. She informed me that I was two minutes late and consequently would appear in front of the prison governor on Monday morning. She didn't mention the smell of alcohol on my breath or say anything about me swaying from side to side; she totally ignored the drink in me. I protested and stood firm, as my watch was telling me that I was on time. I was served an adjudication sheet (also known as a nicking sheet), and I was in front of the governor Monday morning. The governor was known for giving out extra days for sneezing at the wrong time! I wasn't fazed by her, as I knew I was right in my defence. After reading the comments written on the nicking sheet and reading the report that said I had been late retuning to the prison, she asked the two staff members and me to tell her the time on our watches. She also told the time on her watch, and all four of us had different times. After that, she decided that there was no case against me and that there was to be a new rule that everyone who left the prison for rehabilitation, whether a town visit or home leave, must go by the clock at the prison's main gate. That rule is still in place today. I was also home for Christmas that year. I was granted home leave and was able to spend five days with my family. Laura and I went to see a Jamaican artist at the Aston Villa Leisure Centre and I bumped into one of the prison officers from the prison I was currently at. We said our hellos, but I don't know who was more shocked, me or her! That's just one of the many little stories I wanted to share with you to give you an insight into prison life back in 1997.

Chapter Four

THE PRINCE OF DARKNESS

WHILST SERVING MY sentence in the open prison, I received a letter from someone from a prison over in London. This bloke named Daren knew all about me, as he'd heard about the scam with the post office from some guy who was also in prison. Out of curiosity, I replied to this guy, as I was interested in how he had come across my name. I was also very vulnerable but didn't know that at the time. The crime I'd committed was spoken of with admiration in the criminal underworld, and that's how this guy had heard about me. Soon I was in regular contact with this guy, letters going to and fro between us, and before I knew it we had gone from pen pals to lovers through the post! Because there's a lot of jail mail in which women write to men they've met in jail and vice versa, it seemed pretty normal to find a man through the power of the pen. I suppose I became infatuated with this man. I really wanted something that I couldn't have, and that was the attraction if I'm perfectly honest. It wasn't long before we were having inter-prison phone calls. It was the Southeast London accent that did it for me. Stupid, really. When I was released in February 1998, I continued to stay in touch with him through letters and visits. By now he'd been transferred to another jail on the Isle of Wight. I'd been to visit Darren at HMP Camphill a few times. One night I was sat at home when the phone rang and it was him. He was sobbing like a little baby, as he'd just been told one of his older sisters had been found dead on his birthday. He begged me to be there for him at the funeral in London. Although I wasn't really ready to meet the rest of Darren's family under such circumstances, how could I refuse? I was backed into a corner, but what else could I do? I turned up as promised, and he was escorted by two prison officers; he was handcuffed to one of the officers.

The day of his release eventually arrived: 16 December 1998. I went down to London to meet him. (He'd been moved from the Isle of Wight back to HMP Belmarsh, London.) The day Darren got out of jail, I saw him do drugs. The first time I'd seen heroin was in HMP Brockhill. Some bird had been "chasing the dragon"—smoking heroin on a piece of tinfoil. It looked horrible and it stunk of cat wee! I also remember looking at this bird and clearly seeing the devil himself looking back at me! Darren had the same evil look in his eyes. This led to us having a big bust-up in the middle of the street, and he threatened me with all sorts of things. Don't get me wrong; I gave as good as I got, as I am quite a feisty character when the fancy takes me. The fight ended as quickly as it had started. Eventually we were on the coach leaving London heading toward Birmingham to my two-bedroom flat. He'd sworn to me that he had only taken heroin that one time as a stress relief, having just come out of jail and that he wouldn't do it again, especially with what had happened to his sister, and like a prize mug, I really believed him!

My son was now seven years old, but he couldn't get used to living away from his nan and granddad, who lived down the road from our flat. My son made it clear that he didn't like my new partner, and I put it down to him wanting his mom all to himself. I also knew Josh blamed Tony, my ex-partner, for us being separated for my nine-month sentence, as Tony was also involved in the post-office scam. My whole family blamed Tony for leading me astray. In reality, I held all the cards and wasn't the sweet little innocent post office clerk they made me out to be!

Consequently Josh was always at my mom and dad's house, which meant that Darren and I spent a lot of time together alone in the flat. He'd only been out of jail and in my flat for about two weeks before the domestic violence started. The funny thing is that I knew a few women who were victims of domestic violence, and I had always sworn that no man would ever treat me like that, as I wouldn't stand for it. I also thought that with all the hot-blooded males in my family, no man would ever get the chance. But when it happens to you, you're soul-tied to that person and emotionally involved, so you aren't looking at the situation with 20-20 vision as you do when it's somebody else going through the mess. You're practically wearing bifocal specs! It didn't take Darren long to break me down either, as he began with mental torment and progressed to the physical.

I became quite timid in the matter of a few days. It seems quite ironic, really, but the truth is that men like Darren have a game plan, and that is to destroy, destroy a bit more, and then completely destroy. He was a complete control freak. One night out, we went into my dad's regular pub, the Rock, to have a drink. Earlier that night, Darren had back-handed me in the mouth, and my lip was slightly swollen. When my dad saw me, he could see the sorrow in my eyes, and I knew he didn't notice my lip, as it was only slightly swollen. My dad spoke to me in his caring way that only my siblings and I ever see. I lied and put a brave face on and said that I was fine. My dad had always said that he would go to prison for any of his children, and that was running through my mind. My dad didn't like Darren either. Come to think of it, none of my immediate family liked him, but because he was my boyfriend, they accepted him for my sake. If only I had been brave enough to open my mouth and tell someone what had happened, but I wasn't.

Darren travelled to and from London on a regular basis to see his probation officer and his mates. He also signed on the dole in London and told me he would continue to claim his benefits from the benefits office in Woolwich Arsenal. I began working as an area manager for a large cleaning company and enjoyed my job. It didn't bother me that I was working and Darren wasn't, as I realised he was fresh out of jail and had to settle back into the community as best he could. I travelled down to London with him a couple of times to keep him company when I was able to.

Not long after Josh turned eight, we all travelled down to London to spend the week-end and to meet Darren's dad. Darren and I stayed in a bedroom at his dad's flat, and Josh slept on the sofa. Darren's dad seemed a nice man, but he and Darren had a massive row, and this resulted in his dad leaving and saying to Darren, "It's only because there is a lady and a child with you that I haven't thrown you out of my home!" With that his dad left, and we planned to leave Sunday afternoon so that I could return to work on Monday morning and Josh could return to school.

It was late Friday night, and Josh was asleep in the living-room on the sofa while Darren and I sat in the bedroom. Darren began to get some tinfoil out and smooth any creases, flash a lighter flame over the foil, and make a tube. I was mortified watching him, as he performed this action like a real professional. When I asked him what he was doing, he looked at me and said, "I'm making a plate and tube. Why?" He answered me as if I was stupid! I was absolutely gobsmacked! I was forced to take heroin. When I say forced, I mean that he told me for about two hours to just trust him and do it. He threatened me with beatings, which was the easiest of the torments. From what I can remember, he didn't hit me that much; because he'd hit me in the past, the fear of it happening again was terrifying for me, and all he had to do was threaten. The fact that my son was in the other room did bother me, as I didn't want my Josh to hear his mom being traumatised and beaten. When Darren saw I wouldn't be moved, he went straight for the ultimate kill. He threatened to beat my son to a pulp; he knew my boy was my weakest link. After he said that he'd beat my eight-year-old son, fear gripped me by the throat. All this happened in his dad's flat on the Old Kent Road in London. If we'd been in Birmingham, I suppose I would have stood a chance, but with no one to run to in a strange place, I felt I didn't really have a choice. We were on the second floor of a small block of flats alone with something like twelve locks on the front door, and I wasn't going to jump out of a window, although at the time I felt that if my son hadn't been with me, I'd have taken a chance, as anything is better than being with the devil himself. This man claimed he loved me and couldn't understand why I wouldn't make this little sacrifice for him! "All I want you to have is a couple of lines, babe. Just trust me. You'll be fine." I will not say what actual threats he made or the things he said he'd do to my son, as they are too disturbing. He handed me the foil tube, and I tried to make it look like I was inhaling the smoke by sucking through the tube but not actually taking the smoke into my lungs, but he was wise to that. I even got a punch in my mouth for not doing it properly! I can still taste that first bitter taste of heroin in my mouth as I write this. I almost threw up after the first line. He fed me about four lines on a really long sheet of foil. I've heard other users say that after the first taste of heroin, they were instantly hooked. From my experience, I can honestly say that yes, you are hooked after your first encounter. Maybe not everyone becomes instantly addicted, but being instantly hooked and being instantly addicted are two different things in my eyes. Getting hooked simply means you return for the taste and the warm blanket feeling, but being instantly addicted means your body feels it needs it rather than wants it. It's a very powerful drug, because after all Darren said and did to me in the flat that night, I forgave him and didn't blame him for a thing! How sick of me is that? He'd threatened to do physical damage to my boy, he'd done damage to me, and that dirty, stinking devil's dust washed away my parental instincts, emotions, and self respect in a nanosecond. Oh well. What a brilliant way to start a relationship with the devil himself. Little did I know at the time that the abuse hadn't even commenced.

After we'd been together for about six months, we ended up living in southeast London in a one-bedroom flat, but my son stayed with my parents so he could continue to attend his school near to my mom's house. I knew by then I was trapped, and it seemed no one could help me. His idea was to set up home so that Josh could come and live with us. My idea was to wait until he was asleep one night and kill him and be totally free. Yes, even being in jail on a murder charge is freedom compared to being with someone you hate with a burning passion. I knew my son was never going to live with us in London, but I truly believed that one day soon I'd be free and my boy and I could pretend that this nightmare had been just a bad dream. By now I was not only totally a slave to heroin but was also a lover of crack cocaine, and oh boy is that crack in a league of its own when it comes to addictions. I've seen it catch many people from all walks of life by the short and curlys.

From solicitors to bank clerks to police officers, probation officers, common prostitutes, high-class hookers, prison officers, and average housewives. No one is above getting hooked on such powerful drugs. We committed crime to fund our enormous habit. He was always in control. He would place the tube in my mouth and tell me, "All you have to do is suck the smoke into the tube, and I'll do the rest." He even controlled my emotions—what little I had left. I had become numb. I'd gone from a healthy size 10 to a size 0 in a few weeks, my skin was grey and gaunt and in bad condition, my eyes were sunken, and my cheek-bones stood out. He had complete control of my life. He told me to cut my hair quite short, and I felt that I had no choice but to obey him. It was easier that way., I even convinced myself that my hair suited me better now that it was short. I even lied to myself for fear of him. He chased me once to give me a beating because he said it was my fault that the local post office where we needed to go to cash a payment had closed. I tried to run for my life, but he eventually caught up with me, and I was so scared that I actually wet myself!

Another time I was getting ready to go out with him (we went everywhere together), and I was about to curl my hair. He demanded to do it, as I was his property. As he brought the tongs close to my forehead I flinched. He got angry, saying he wouldn't burn me with the tongs. He brought them close to my scalp a second time, and he did burn me that time. Admittedly it was a genuine accident, but he said that he hadn't touched my forehead and that I was exaggerating and that if there was not a burn on my forehead after the way I'd carried on, then I would pay for trying to make him feel guilty. I thanked God that a burn mark appeared on my forehead ten minutes later!

When I look back at the things I went through with this man, I know I'm truly blessed to be alive to tell this story. There were loads of times that man hit me and abused me, and you're probably asking yourself,

"Why didn't she go back to her family?" it's because pride is one of the biggest and most powerful weapons in the demonic kingdom, and the spirits of pride and fear dwelt in me to the fullest. My pride couldn't take my parents seeing me like this. I was also very embarrassed. Some may ask, "Why didn't she go to the police?" When you live in the dark on drugs and crime, the police can be your number-one enemy. No, I was too far gone in this dark drug lifestyle, and I believed that I would have to grin and bear it, as this was my life and I had to get on with it. I had never loved this man; in fact, I hated him with a burning passion so intense I could taste it. If you've ever been ruled by fear, then you know where I'm coming from. He used to give me pedicures and manicures, style my hair, and tell me what to wear and how to wear it, but these apparently nice acts were all done to increase my fear and his control. There was also a time before we moved to London when I had a bad pain in my back. I was standing in the kitchen complaining that my back was hurting. He said that I must take one of his antibiotics that his GP had given him. I told him that I could not take them, as I only had to say the word *antibiotic* and I got thrush. He insisted that I take a couple and that I'd be fine. He bullied me into taking this medication. It's the way he did it that still angers me to this day. He crushed the tablet and got a glass of fresh orange juice and put the powder into the juice. I protested and told him I would get thrush, but he ignored me. The following morning I woke up to discover that I had thrush! When I told him, he got mad at me and said that I was only telling him that to make him feel bad! Mental torture is a terrible thing. He possessed me, and as I was weak and vulnerable, I allowed it to happen. I felt as if I were living in hell on earth and nobody could help me.

One day we were on our way back from his dad's flat, and we had a car parked in the car-park near the flats. The car was not running, so he decided to tow it back to the flat we lived in. Darren was in a transit van and had the rope to tow the car back home. He told me to sit in the car, turn the key to unlock the steering wheel, and to leave a bit of slack to allow the van to pull the car without the rope snapping. Easy! It would have been if I had been living in a relaxed body, but whenever that man told me to do something, fear of getting it wrong gripped me with such a force that I shook. In other words, I was a nervous wreck. He was my master and I was his slave, and he spoke to me as if I were a child. He was a nasty piece of work. We set off, and I got it wrong a couple of times, but he didn't blow his lid. I gained a bit of confidence after we'd been driving for about twenty minutes and couldn't wait to get back to the flat, as I wanted some gear. He spotted a mate and pulled over to talk. We sat for a few minutes while he spoke to his mate, so I took the key out of the ignition and waited for him to finish his chat. It all happened so quickly. He jumped back into the van, started up the engine, and began to take off. I panicked, as the key wouldn't turn in the ignition. The next thing I knew, the front wheel on the driver side burst as it went over a Ballard, and then the wheel at the rear of the car also on the driver side also burst. I was shouting out of the window to get his attention, but he wasn't looking. He looked through his rear mirror as we approached a junction. When he saw what had happened, he flew out of the van and came to the car swearing and waving his arms about. I tried to explain what had happened, but it fell on deaf ears. He wasn't interested in what I had to say; he was wound up, and I was getting the blame. He was absolutely demented! He began swearing at me and called me all the stupid cows under the sun. (I didn't know there were that many species of cows until that day). He began dragging me out of the car. Naturally, I tried to resist but failed miserably. Other motorists saw the commotion, and some shouted abuse at him for ill-treating a woman. The traffic came to a halt, and there was a lot of angry motorists. The men shouted at him to leave me alone and to pick on a man rather than a woman, but he didn't have anything to say to other men. He said to me that he believed that these men were lovers of mine, as they had no business getting involved with domestics. I wanted to tell the men in their cars to keep out of it, as it was making matters worse for me, although I know that if I'd done that, it would have made matters worse all around. He told me that this wasn't over and that when we get home I'd get the beating of my life. I was petrified.

Chapter Five

THE DAY I TOOK CONTROL

WE GOT HOME, and the abuse started as soon as we stepped into our "love nest." I then realised that this man was truly mad, sick in the head! When the abuse stopped, I looked at him coldly and said, "That is the last time you ever hit me again. Do you understand?" I must have said it with a conviction that warranted his full attention, as I saw great fear in his eyes. It must have registered, as he didn't hit me again for a few weeks. That's when I tasted pure hate, because I understood that he *could* control his outbursts of anger. In that split second, my fear turned into hate, and I really don't know which of the two is worse! He came at me a few weeks after my warning, and I picked up a hammer that was on the floor by the sofa and whacked him on the hip. He was in shock and stood stock still, and I knew he had been given a dose of his own medicine. He was thick, because he went for me again a few days later. The hammer had been removed from the living-room, and he obviously thought I'd got brave for just one day, so you can imagine his reaction when I jumped up and flew back at him. All fear of him left my body as I took his power from him. I picked up an ornament and smashed it with force over his head. He cowered like a baby and shook with fear. He had dreadlocks which were thick and covered his skull, so why was he on the verge of tears? I lost control and began to really go for him. I screamed at him, "Why are you crying baby? Surely this is nothing compared to what you've put me through!" I began smashing the flat to pieces, windows included. He sat in the armchair cowering and covering his head in his arms. Pathetic! I was in such a rage that I blacked out for a few minutes. I then realised that this joke called a relationship was in a very dangerous place. I now had control of the situation. He begged me and said that if I wanted to go back to Birmingham I had his permission. He really didn't get it, did he? If he thought for one second that I was about to walk away and leave him after what he'd done to me, he was stupider than I thought. No, this was payback time, and until I'd given him the torment and walking-on-egg-shells treatment he'd so easily given to me, I wasn't going anywhere. Anyway, who would keep me? I'd become completely dependent on him, as he held the golden key to my drug addiction. I spent the night at a mate's house and returned the next day for my daily fix, as my life depended on it. The fact that he had given me his permission to go back to Birmingham made me even more determined to stay just to prove to myself that I would no longer take any suggestion or command from this pathetic excuse for a man. I was no longer under lock and key. His telling me I was free to go was another way of saying, "I no longer have control over you," and I needed to stay around and prove that to him and to myself! It was very self-destructive, but I failed to see it that way, as the drugs had really blocked my vision.

I couldn't leave now, as I was totally trapped by the drugs, and the damage that man had done to my soul was not going to be mended for a long while. He had completely destroyed me with the drugs and the abuse I had endured on a regular basis. Did you know that when you're hooked on drugs the devil has hold of your soul? The devil also has hold of your emotions when you're a slave to him through heroin. I wasn't going to walk out just like that. Not only had he taken total control of my life and made me totally dependent on him, but I really felt that I couldn't just go back to Birmingham in the state I was in. I was ashamed and believed I'd be judged and there would be lots of "I told you so." I wasn't going anywhere. All I wanted to do now was take back what was rightfully mine—my self-respect and dignity. He'd got me on hard drugs, and I needed him to keep on supporting me; after all, he had got me hooked. He could keep me but on my terms. I'd just become every man's worst nightmare! After all that happened that day, I believe the devil himself placed a ring on my finger for life, because something entered my body. I went from frightened-for-her-life Mandy to all-I-want-is-drugs-and-my-power-back Mandy. On that night when I walked out to go spend the night at a mate's house, something massive changed in both of our lives.

The following morning I had to return, as he had the drugs and I wanted some. After I'd had my fix, I just acted as if nothing had happened, but we both knew that something had taken place, and he was in a very dangerous position. As I only weighed about six stone, I thought I'd get myself sorted, start eating properly, and then go home to my parents and son—but not until I'd made his life complete hell for a while so that he'd have an idea what it was like to be on edge all the time!

The only weight I added to my body came in the form of the ounces of heroin I picked up from our main supplier. At this point in our sad, sorry lives, we were making a lot of money through selling drugs. I became a secret crack smoker, as he'd eased off the crack cocaine and mostly smoked heroin. So I'd sneak out with about £150.00 per day to smoke crack in and around London. I smoked everywhere except at home unless it was really late at night; then I sneaked into the bathroom and locked myself in and smoked my drugs. There was even a time when I was so out of it that I got into the bath one night and woke up at around 9.30 a.m. the following morning! Whenever I think of that time, I recognise that I was the recipient of outrageous grace. We were making more than £1,000.00 a day selling heroin. I took charge to begin with, and when we got really busy, I handed the reins over to him. I still sold drugs, but only on the rare occasions when a customer was considered dangerous. The reason I served this type of punter was that they trusted me, as they had only dealt with me when we first started selling. Darren also felt intimidated by anyone stronger than him!

One day I woke up from having a dream about police officers arresting him outside of the pub where we used to meet our punters who bought our wraps of heroin. The dream seemed so real that I was talking in my sleep, and he woke me up and asked what I was dreaming about. I told him about the dream and advised him that we should be more vigilant, as I believed that the dream was a sign. Later that day we got raided, but we were waiting for the police, as we acted on my vision. As you can imagine, the boys in blue were a bit pissed to say the least. They found no heroin but found some cannabis which he planted in the house to deter the drug dog, and it worked. He was taken to the police station and had to pay a £25.00 fine.

Another time when we were in the famous flat, there was a knock at the door and it was a so-called mate of his with some random guy I'd never seen before in my life who had a sawn-off shotgun. I screamed, and I'd be lying if I said I wasn't scared. Well, wouldn't you be with a sawn-off in your face? They made up some cock-and-bull story to rob him. This is what happens when you keep company with down-and-out crack-heads. Most of the time I was out having the time of my life with my drug associates. I make it sound really interesting and glamorous, but let me tell you how glamorous it really was. I would wake up at the crack of dawn with a foil tube in my mouth and a large amount of heroin melted on the foil plate. I'd then get totally smashed until I couldn't keep my eyes open. Then it was time for a bit of crack to liven me up a bit. Off I'd go to meet the crack dealer and find a staircase in a deserted block of flats or sit in my car and smoke a twenty shot (£20.00 worth). I'd then either immediately go back to the dealer and score more crack or come back down with heroin; about £20.00 worth would do it. I'd then score a lump of crack, say £100.00 worth, and go to a drug house, where I'd give the person who lived at the house a nice smoke, and that would secure me a seat for the duration until my drugs ran out. It'd be late evening now, so I'd score another £50.00 worth of crack to see me through the night. The beauty of selling heroin when you're an addict is that you don't have to go and score it, as it's there on tap. I often didn't know what time it was, and sometimes I didn't know what day it was either. Most nights I'd be up smoking crack and heroin until early hours, and that was why I was always up at the crack of dawn—because I never really slept. I was out of my face twenty-four seven. Occasionally I'd have what I used to call an early night, meaning about 2.00 a.m. If this sounds glamorous to anyone, then they really need to invest in a dictionary and look up the true meaning of *glamorous*!

As time went by, there were about six other drug raids, but the police had bad timing; if they ever found anything, it was only a couple of wraps which we claimed as personal. On the seventh raid, the police force's hard work paid off. They're persistent; I'll say that about them! Just before the police came through the door, Darren threw a weight of gear out of the window, and then he decided to follow it. He legged it, leaving me in the flat to face the Old Bill! They recovered some of the heroin, and had to charge someone, and as I was the only person in the flat, that someone had to be me. They knew that he'd jumped out of the window, as he'd left it wide open. I didn't think to close the window, as I was in shock, and the neighbour below took pleasure in telling the police that he'd had it on his toes. They also found a double-barrelled shotgun in the bedroom, which I said I didn't know anything about, and they actually believed me and said they'd be asking Darren about it when they caught up with him. They knew he'd been in prison for possession of a firearm in the past. The fact that I was in the flat when the raid took place meant that I was also charged for possession with intent to supply. I was taken to the police station, where I gave a no-comment interview and was released the next morning. I found it strange that I was charged and then released but then realised that the police only gave me bail because they knew I would know where to find Darren and wanted me to lead them to him. Of course when I did see him, we both realised why the police had bailed me, but he said he would hand himself in and take the charge. We only lasted a few days out together, as the person whose house we were staying at couldn't take the way Darren spoke to him in his own home and went to the police and informed them of his whereabouts. The police came crashing through the door early on a Monday morning and took Darren to the police station to question him about the raid that had taken place in our flat. I was due to appear in court a few days after his arrest, as I had been granted police bail. However, due to my drug-fuelled lifestyle, I failed to appear at court. Consequently, I was on the run. A few weeks later I was arrested and remanded in police custody.

I was brought before Woolwich Magistrate Court the following day and remanded in custody on bail to reappear for sentencing. The CPS charged me with possession with intent of a controlled class A drug. I was looking at quite a lengthy prison sentence.

There was a woman whom I met whilst on remand at HMP Holloway who informed me of another inmate who had an uncle who was in the Freemasons. I'd heard a couple of things about the Freemasons regarding the criminal justice system. I was led to believe that they were an organisation where special handshakes took place that allowed some criminals to get a lesser sentence or none at all. I'd practiced contacting spirits through clairvoyance, and I diligently sought the angels of darkness, as I had to find out about this code. I really didn't fancy doing a few years in jail. The night before I was due in court for sentencing, I entered the spirit realm and contacted the demons who roam late at night (also known as ghosts); I was shown a sign and told how to do it. The spirit told me to do the sign there and then, so I did. Let me explain. That is what seeking the powers of darkness is all about. I was given a sign by my demonic agent. I performed the sign before the judge, who was known for being very harsh with sentencing, and he began to stutter after I made the sign, so I made it again, and he started to panic and stumble over his words. I couldn't believe it. He said that this case should go to Crown Court, but he dealt with me by giving me a four-month custodial sentence! Was the sign I performed the sign that is used by a Freemason member? I don't know but what I do know is the sign I did got me a reduced prison sentence. I know that when a lot of people heard of my sentence, they immediately thought I was a police informer, as such a sentence is far too light for such a crime. At the time, I would rather have had people think that of me even though the truth is I invoked spirits to save my skin. People wouldn't have believed me, as the judge in question was well known for giving out harsh sentences for minor offences. I will talk about this more in another book concerning my true experiences of walking with dark power. I was given a four-month custodial sentence, and as I'd spent a few weeks in custody already, I didn't have very much left to do. My release date was set for mid-December that year.

Chapter Six

RETURNING HOME TO BIRMINGHAM

EVENTUALLY I WAS released from prison and went to stay at a mate's house in Catford, London. She was also a drug addict, and consequently we sat and smoked heroin and crack cocaine until the early hours of the morning. Although I came out of prison drug free and had no withdrawal symptoms, mentally I was still very much addicted. A lot of people don't understand the intense power of certain drugs and the strong hold they can have over your life.

Thankfully my older brother managed to contact me, and we arranged for me to go back home to my family, who were very worried about my welfare. I wanted to be home for Christmas.

I returned to my mom and dad's on Christmas Eve 2000. It was very emotional seeing my long-lost family after what seemed a lifetime. It was too painful to put into words, especially when I saw my baby after being apart for so long.

It didn't take long before I was caught up in the rat race and was using drugs even more than I had when I lived in London. I cashed one of my younger brother's GIRO payments with the intention of replacing the money as soon as I had a smoke of heroin as I was detoxing but he was informed by the post office when he enquired about his missing GIRO. The guilt I felt was unbearable, but because I did a couple of things that people do when they're sold out to heroin and crack, I felt as if I had murdered someone. That was often the way I felt whilst taking those drugs. Truth be told, I probably would have found it easier to live with murder than the hurt I put my family through. Before I knew it, I was shoplifting giant legs of lamb, joints of beef, and so on. I soon moved on to bigger things, such as clothing from fashion shops. I'd been caught shoplifting a few times and had been given fines and community rehabilitation orders, but none of them seem to work for me at that time. I got sent to HMP Brockhill, Redditch. I was there from November 2001 and was in a cell next door to a woman whom I'd met in prison back in 1997 when I was in for the post office theft. We got on pretty well. My mate had converted to the Islamic religion and told me things about her religion. She encouraged me to give up crime and the lifestyle that came with it and become a Muslim. However, when heroin came into the jail, we took it and abused it.

She showed me how to pray correctly to Allah and explained how to do the *wuju* (the wash before you can pray). She also told me how many times a day one is expected to pray and showed me the prayers that one must pray to worship. I read through the prayers and wanted to find out more about this religion, as it sounded very easy. She told me that the Qur'an was written in the same language all over the world and said that the Bible contradicts itself and has many translations; that, she said, was one of the reasons people don't understand it. Because I was very confused by the Bible growing up and didn't really understanding the distinctions between God, Jesus, the Lord, and the Holy Spirit, when she told me that Muslims pray directly to Allah, who is their God, it all seemed much easier to me. In the past, I had stayed away from all this religion stuff because it seemed too confusing. I was learning the main prayer in English, but then my mate told me that the prayer was void unless it was spoken in Arabic. As I was so determined to say this prayer, I asked her to speak the prayer in Arabic, and I wrote it out as it was pronounced. For two days I sat and practiced the prayer in Arabic, and after those forty-eight hours I had learned the main prayer so that I could pray correctly to Allah. I was sceptical, because there's no way you can put your heart into something you don't feel in your heart, but she told me that you can only pray that way to draw closer to Allah. I was told that the good thing about this prayer was that anything you asked for would be done. But how could I ask for anything that I truly desired if I wasn't allowed to ask from my heart in the language that I have spoken all my life? So this religious thing was confusing me again! So let me get this right—if you don't pray in Arabic, then your prayer is void? By now I'd gone from confused to confused.com! Something inside of me knew that there was a God and that He accepts our prayers no matter what language we speak in. The discipline in the Islamic religion is intense, as you have to pray at certain times every day. Now let's move on.

I was released from HMP Brockhill on 7 March 2002. The next day I went to the local hospital to visit my nan (my mom's mom), as she had been diagnosed with cancer. The family had been told that nan only had a few days left, and we were very upset, to say the least. Nan stayed with us for a lot longer than the doctor predicted. On 17 April 2002, Nan took her last breath. We were all devastated at the loss. I was with her as she took her last, precious breath. I found it quite painful, but I also felt relief, as Nan was a staunch Christian, and although I didn't believe in Jesus Christ, I believed that she had gone to a better place. Just when I thought nothing could get worse, my Granny Tweed died nine weeks later, also of cancer. Losing both grandmothers in a matter of nine weeks to cancer was devastating.

When I first came out of prison, I managed to stay focused and didn't really do drugs. I dabbled (dabbling means doing drugs on a part-time basis), but after the death of both my grandmothers, I went off the rails, as I found the pressure too much. Losing one nan was traumatising. When my mommy (my dad's mum who I fondly called mommy) also went, I thought I was going to lose my mind. No one had any idea of the damage that did to me. I woke up with pain in my heart first thing in the morning and real tears filled my eyes. Then I'd remember something about her just by looking at my dad, as he resembled her so much, and I'd fill up with tears all over again. I wept myself to sleep some nights.

On the day of her funeral, I stood over her open coffin, and my tears ran down my cheeks uncontrollably. I wet her lifeless body with the tears of true love. One of my aunts had to prise me away so that the undertaker could replace the lid to her coffin so that she could be taken to her final resting place. Not long after Mommy's funeral, my drug habit escalated to another level—a level that I had to maintain, as withdrawing is painful. When you withdraw from drugs not only do your emotions hit you hard but your body is screaming in pain until you get that next fix. I still prayed to Allah, so in effect I was practising Islam for a few months after my release in March of that year.

From 2002 to 2010, I was in and out of prison more times than I care to remember; however, that won't stop me from sharing some of the things I saw and did whilst I toured some of England's women's prisons.

Almost every time I got arrested and sent to jail, I either had a parcel of heroin with me or met another inmate with a parcel of gear on her. Does the saying "the devil looks after his own" spring to mind? I recall being sent to HMP Brockhill, and because I was on the run, I always had my gear with me. I was sent to jail and had something like eleven wraps of heroin on me. I made it my business to find out who was already locked up so I could have a little wrap for them when I had my welcome party. I arrived at the prison when all the other girls were banged up for the night, which meant I had to become a window warrior for the night. I got talking to a girl who was on the same wing as me, but she was upstairs on the second level. When I realised that we were from the same area and knew each other, she made a swing using a tea-pack bag (one of the brown paper bags that the prison canteen put our daily tea-bags, sugar, and whiteners in) and a dressing-gown belt and lowered the bag down to me. I popped a jail wrap in the bag, and she pulled it up to her window, and Bob's your uncle!

I recall going to HMP Eastwood Park a few times too. There was always someone on the induction wing with a parcel. If it wasn't me, then another girl would have a parcel in their possession. The screws were wise to the goings-on on the wing but were limited as to what they could do. As drugs stay in the body for a few days, we weren't drug tested when we were first brought in, which gave us time to have a good boot and not get added grief. The amount of drugs I witnessed in that jail alone was phenomenal.

The time I spent in jail wasn't always focused on drugs. Some of the things that happened behind prison walls were funny! I will always recall the times when we were allowed to have karaoke. I was an MC and my MC name was Gangsta. That became my nickname within the criminal world. I wasn't shy about grabbing the mike and being the centre of attention. There were lots of talented women in prison with voices that would put a lot of pop stars to shame. I found that there was always someone who was good at arts also. Looking back at some of the women that I did time with, a lot of them were lost souls caught up in the rat race because of the cares of the world, and it was a real eye-opener.

I met a lot of girls whilst I toured. There's a funny tale to tell from almost every prison sentence I did. There was a time when I was off my face on heroin and I had the bright idea to sue the prison service. I had a boot during the night and was absolutely smashed. When I woke up the next day, I was still out of my head, as the drug was pretty potent. I wanted to get out of my cell for one reason or another, so I filled a jug from the tap and tipped the water onto the floor, got my mate to press the cell bell, and lay on the floor groaning and holding my left side. The officer who came to our cell was an old-school screw. He rolled his eyes at my performance and said, "Up you get, Tweed. The act's over." I pretended to be dazzled as if I had been knocked unconscious, but he decided to allow me to have my moment and waited patiently. My speech was slurred, because I really was high on the drugs from the night before. My mate helped me up, but she was having trouble keeping her face serious. Then I began limping on my left leg, but I had my hand on the right side of my back. The screw looked at me, and he couldn't help but laugh, saying, "How did you end up on the floor?" I said that I'd slipped and landed on my left side and banged my head and I wanted a doctor. I looked a complete idiot, as I was limping on the wrong foot, my T-shirt was wet on the right side, and the puddle of water on the floor was in the wrong place to match my story! I got to see the doctor and got some strong painkillers, but the screw laughed at my attempt to lodge an official complaint!

I was also famous for making toast in my cell with a taper (tissue paper made into a wick and then set alight with a lighter or matches).

I would stand and cook toast in my cell, filling the prison wing with the smell of toast. A few screws tried to catch me in the act but were always too late, apart from one screw who nobody really liked—there was always one. I was making toast in my cell, and this officer walked in and caught me buttering my freshly cooked toast. Rather than leave me alone with my breakfast, he decided to tackle me. He went to grab my toast, and I quickly moved my hand. We played the cat-and-mouse game of him trying to get my toast and me not giving it over. In the end, he gave me a warning for making toast in my cell, but I had the last laugh: I kept my toast and ate it!

When I tell you that there are people from all walks of life behind bars, I'm not kidding you. One of the most disturbing sentences I did was in 2000 in Holloway. There was a woman who was on remand for the murder of her daughter. She denied killing her child and was always very timid when walking around the prison until one day another inmate pushed in front of her whilst we queued for our dinner. She turned on the queue jumper nastily, and everyone who witnessed it was shocked. She also walked around telling anyone who'd listen to her about her baby, who had dropped dead outside of a church. Someone told me that she was innocent, and I had to ask her myself. Her story set off alarm bells in my head, but if you saw how humble, shy, and extremely good natured she appeared to be, you too would have been led to believe that she was another innocent woman locked away for a crime she didn't commit. Her story was that she had been in church and her daughter had been misbehaving, so she had smacked her, and because her daughter had dropped to the floor and died outside of the church that day, other church members had reported her to the police and said that she'd hit the child, causing her death. That's what set the alarm bells off in my head. She had photos of her and her daughter, and yes, they looked very happy together. She always walked around the prison with her Bible gripped tightly under her arm, and sometimes she had photos of the little girl who had died.

I had been to court and was in reception having a meal and waiting to be taken back to my cell when she sat opposite me. She had some photos on the dining table and was admiring them and telling me that she missed her baby. It was quite emotional for me. I don't recall the reason, but at one point some of us were to lodge over night in different cells on different wings, and I was put in a four-bed cell with this woman and two others. I knew one of the women, as I had shared a cell with her when I first came to HMP Holloway in September of that year, so we were having a natter and a laugh about prison life. The next thing I knew, this lady who was on a murder charge was standing by the cell door speaking to an officer. I couldn't hear what she was saying, as she spoke softly. However, I clearly heard the officer reply something like, "You'll have to go one night without it; I'm not going to bring you another one!" I was gobsmacked when I heard the way this officer spoke to the woman, because this particular officer was very fair and very professional and more often than not had a kind word for us girls. I then found out that the woman had left her Bible in reception and was requesting a Bible for the night. So why was this officer so rude to her? I slept peacefully that night.

A few days later when I was back on my allocated wing, I was chilling on my bed. An officer came into my cell and took our little portable radio which was on a table. I wondered what was going on at first, but I found out later that all the radios and newspapers around the prison were confiscated that day, so obviously there was something happening in the outside world that they didn't want us to hear about.

I was attending Woolwich Magistrates court a few days later when I realised that something was very wrong. There were about seventy women in the changing area all wearing bright blue prison dressing gowns and flip-flops and waiting to be searched before we were led out of the prison. After what seemed an age, I was seated on the sweat box (the van that transfers prisoners to and from the courts). I sat in front of a girl who I knew from my time in jail. We were talking in what's known as back slang. I had smuggled a lighter past the screws, and she wanted a light for her roll-up. I put it under my door and was just about to slide the lighter to her when a black boot gently trod on my fingers. When I looked up to see an officer smiling down at me, I told her to get her boot off my hand. She removed her foot but was still standing outside my door. The girl behind me started shouting to a woman who was sitting quietly at the rear of the bus. She was situated so that there wasn't a prisoner in the cubicle opposite hers. The girl behind asked the silent woman in the rear cubicle various questions, such as, "When did you come on the bus, love? How come you're in the corner hidden away from the rest of us? What's the big secret?" The woman wouldn't answer the questions. I then discovered that it was the woman who was on remand for the murder of her daughter. She had been put on the bus first while the rest of us were waiting in our dressing-gowns to be searched. I said to the girl behind me, "She's accused of killing her daughter, but she didn't do it." I was convinced that she hadn't murdered her daughter, because I had been told by a fellow inmate that she had documentation from an outside doctor stating that her daughter had collapsed and died from an illness that had gone undetected while the child was alive. I called out to the woman and asked her if she was all right. She didn't answer me. The officer appeared in front of me and asked me why I was asking the woman if she was all right. I said, "Because she's innocent. She didn't do it." The officer slid a newspaper under my door and said, "How can you call what she done innocent?" I read the article in the paper regarding the woman's charge, but it didn't say anything I didn't know. The reporter had made her sound guilty already!

That was the day I received my four-month custodial sentence, and I'd done a few weeks on remand, so I didn't have long left to serve. I got transferred to HMP Highpoint a few days after being sentenced. Numerous prisoners told me that a well-known convicted child murderer who'd committed a string of offences with her partner back in the 1970s was down the block, but I didn't see her. I'm sharing this bit of information with you to show that I was in jail with people from all walks of life.

When I was back in Birmingham after Christmas in 2000, I sat watching the news with tears streaming down my face. They were tears of anger and deep sorrow mixed together. There on my mom's wide-screen TV was a photograph of the little girl that I had seen whilst I was in HMP Holloway a few weeks before. The nice lady with the Bible was described as an evil aunt who had murdered her niece who had been sent to England from France to have a better life. This woman had been successful at fooling social services, and the news pointed this information out as a fact. If I hadn't met the woman myself, I'd probably have shared the majority opinion of the country, which held that social services had failed this child and had chosen to ignore the warning signs. This woman was a very calm and placid person. I've always had a sixth sense, and even though I had my suspicions about the way the supposedly nice woman told her story about how her daughter had dropped dead outside of her local church, and even though I had seen a nasty side to her that day when the other inmate had pushed in front of her, and even though I had seen the officers treat her like trash, and despite the fact she didn't acknowledge me when I called out to her on the sweat box, her body language told a totally different story. I can see how she fooled social services. I must stress that this woman had the whole jail fooled, and most of the women there were hardened criminals who did not miss a trick. This woman was found guilty of murder. Sometimes in prison you don't know who your next-door neighbour is.

All sorts of things ran through my mind after watching the news. I was angry, because when I replayed the encounters I had had with this woman and saw how she was, I was disturbed. Of course there was nothing I could have done that would have brought that little girl back into the world, but I did wonder what I would have done if I'd known the full story when I had to sleep in a bed next to that woman. I think a lot of women would be asking themselves the very same question.

On the whole, I found that prison can either make you or break you. It made me stronger in the sense that I got hardened to prison life, and sometimes I looked forward to a bit of rehab. It was the one time my family could be certain that I was not on the street or dead in a gutter. My mom told me once that my dad was tormented by the thought that the police would knock the door one night and ask him to come and identify my dead body. So I can confirm that my family slept easier at night when I was behind bars, as they knew where I was morning, noon, and night. I've always looked at jail as easy, but I have come to realise it's easier for the hardened criminal; I was in and out of jail for years and became comfortable with it. However, I was very selfish in that respect, because I have it on good authority that it wasn't easy for my family. Because my drug habit was a big one, I welcomed jail, and I still believe that going to jail so often saved my life, because many times I was knocking on death's door.

The last time I was sentenced and sent to prison was on 28 October 2010. The weird thing is that I had a strange feeling that this was my last time in shackles. I was only doing a six-month sentence, so it was a short stay. I started my sentence in HMP Fostonhall in Derbyshire.

After I'd been there for a few weeks, I was transferred to HMP Drakehall. I met some really good girls on that sentence. There was a Nigerian woman who everyone called Mommy, as she was the mothering type. She was an inspiration to us all. She was a very spiritual woman who prayed for me when I was at the gates the morning that I was being released. She held on to me and prayed in a bear whisper and would not let me go. She had tears in her eyes, and I knew that whatever she prayed for me was deep. I can tell you that the girls who were in Exeter House over Christmas and New Year will have a few stories to tell their grandchildren in years to come. Let's just say that we welcomed 2011 with a bang! We didn't get back to the house until 3 a.m. New Year's Day! We also had parties, watched DVDs on the weekend, and were there for each other. It wasn't just some of the girls who were in Exeter House that I rolled with. There were a few girls spread out over the jail that I became good mates with. We had a special bond, and the night before I went home, we had an invitation-only leaving party. I was a first-class comic; no wonder I was called Prankster and not Gangsta sometimes! I'd studied a handful of characters within the jail and decided to put on a show by mimicking their traits. I know that night is still talked about today, as it was a leaving party none of the girls will ever forget!

I slept like a baby the night before I was released. After I'd said all my good-byes and done a lot of crying, I was released from HMP Drakehall on 27 January 2011. Eventually I was on the train on my way to Birmingham. I had a very strange feeling. I knew something was going to happen, but I couldn't put my finger on it. Whilst in prison I had been on a methadone script, and I had done a detox programme to come off the green liquid, which meant that for the last three to four weeks of my sentence, I was completely drug free. However, I felt ill, as I was still withdrawing. It's a slow and painful process, so basically I still felt like crap. I didn't have a strong urge to go and get drugs immediately after release, and that was very strange. As soon as I met up with my mate Doug, a drug addict, I wanted to get off my face. I scored some crack and heroin, and we went to his flat and smoked all afternoon and all night. I was supposed to go to a shared accommodation to reside, as I was homeless, but Doug said I could stay over at his on the sofa and if I still wanted to go to the hostel the following day he'd drop me over, as he knew the area well.

The following morning I woke up and felt very rough. I had smoked a lot of drugs, and I'd drunk a bottle of Irish cream. It's a wonder I woke up at all. When I woke up that morning, I heard another person's voice. I went to the bathroom, and when I came out I saw a man sitting with my mate smoking heroin. He offered me some, but I said no thanks. I wanted to kick myself for refusing, but there was definitely something in me that wanted to get away from the drugs at that particular time. I had no idea what it was; I just knew that it wasn't my strength or my will.

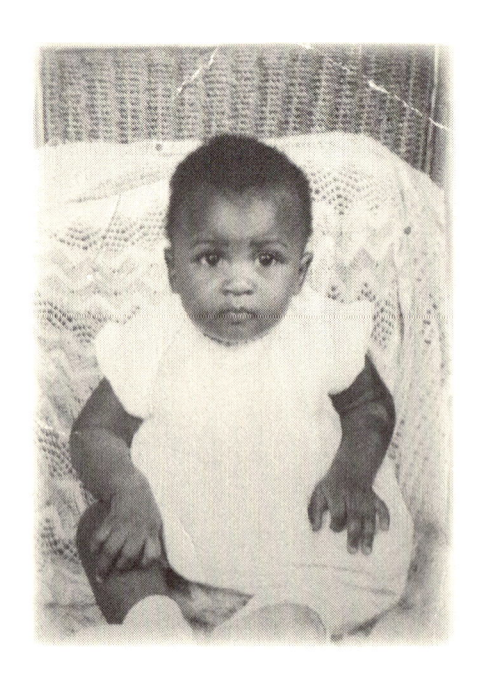

Lovely baby Amanda 9 months old

Amanda 4 months before the drugs

Amanda released from Prison January 2011

Brooke House the Miracle House

Mrs Jarvis

Victoria James Director, Brooke House

Pastors David & Yvonne Jarvis

The Discipleship Class Members at Brooke House

Lisa Foad, Tina James, Rita Clarke and Amanda Tweed
on Mothers Day March 2012

Dr Stephen Richards, founder LOMI
celebrating the fourth year in ministry

Church Members and Pastor David Jarvis to the far right

Amanda ministering in Church

Chapter Seven

THE HAND OF GOD

WE MADE OUR way over to Erdington, Birmingham, and I came to a place called Brooke House on Slade Road. As soon as I walked in the door, I had a feeling of calm and tranquillity, but I couldn't explain it in words. The lady who owned the premises came out of her office to meet and greet me. I instantly felt power coming from this woman, but it wasn't the power I recognised. The spirit that was in me tried to reject her, and I recall saying to her, "I can see through people," warning her that I was Gangsta. She looked straight back at me and said, "I too can see through people," and I knew she wasn't lying. I didn't like her, but I was drawn to her, and it threw me off guard. She didn't rise up to me, and she didn't back down either. I didn't know what was happening, but I knew it was a force stronger than my own. I was used to people having respect for me or totally disliking me. I've heard people say, "Like her or hate her; either way you have to rate her," referring to me and my drug lifestyle.

A resident who introduced herself as Elaine showed me around the shared house and then showed me to studio 1, which was where my bed awaited. As soon as I stepped foot in that room, I knew that I wouldn't be doing drugs there, but not because of the smoke alarm or anything physical. It was spiritual, but I didn't know what it was at the time. It was a strange feeling I felt in that house, but I couldn't quite understand what was going on.

I had planned to go shoplifting with my mate Doug, but I wanted to go out alone. It was a selfish desire, but I didn't need him with me—it was extra money I'd have to pay out, and I was quite sick of supporting men with drug habits. However, we went out as planned, but after I'd sold my stuff I didn't have the strong urge to score drugs. When I was around Doug, for some unknown reason I didn't like it, because he reminded me of heroin and crack. He hadn't done anything wrong; in fact, he said that he didn't want drugs that day too, so he dropped me off and I cooked myself a meal and stayed indoors. I used tinfoil to aid me when I shoplifted, and the sight of the foil would trigger me to think of heroin and crack cocaine, but that day it had no mental effect on me. In all the years that I smoked heroin, the sight of foil had automatically triggered my brain to think about the drugs. That day, the thought didn't come into my mind. I thought it was strange, but I didn't dwell on it too much. The following day I woke up expecting to feel really ill and needing and wanting a smoke of brown, but I felt calm and at peace with no detox symptoms. Doug came around to pick me up, but I was on the sofa in the residential lounge with my quilt draped over me, and I told him that I didn't want to go out grafting that day. After he'd gone with a bee in his bonnet, I got ready and went out shoplifting alone. He really reminded me of drugs, and I couldn't stand being around him for that reason. Something was happening to me, and I had no control over this change whatsoever. The next day I did the same: I went shoplifting, sold my things, made my money, and came back to the shared house and chilled for the night. The following day I got up early, got dressed, and went to the phone box to call him to let him know I wasn't going out grafting again, but I could tell by his voice that he wasn't happy. When I was out shoplifting, the sight of the tinfoil and the drug dealers' mobile numbers stored in my phone had absolutely no effect on me whatsoever. I went out on my travels, made my money, and returned to Brooke House. When I returned that night, Elaine, another resident, told me that my mate Doug had turned up whilst I was out, let himself onto the property, and had been just about to walk straight into my room when Mrs Jarvis (the founder of Brooke House) saw him and told him to get off her premises. When I heard that, I knew that he wouldn't be back, and I thought, "Go on, Mrs J!"

I felt that there was something about Mrs Jarvis. We didn't hit it off when we first met, but I had a grudging respect for her. I couldn't put my finger on what it was about this lady. I knew she was a Christian, and you could feel love coming off her in big waves, but we didn't connect spiritually. One of our first real conversations was about the church that she attended, and my immediate response was to tell her that I didn't do church. She just smiled at me and said OK. The other residents had told me that you had to attend church or else you'd be asked to leave! I was shocked, and I waited for the woman to tell me this as well. Not everyone who lived in Brooke House attended church, so that turned out not to be true. I also never heard her say that to anyone, so I saw it as idle gossip. She did mention God to me once, and my immediate response was, "I'm a Muslim." I wasn't, but it was the only religion I'd really had anything to do with, so I used it as a tool.

After I'd been in Brooke House for about a week, I settled into a routine of waking up at 7 a.m., showering, dressing, and going out on my shoplifting mission. One day I woke up with the intention to go out as normal, but my body wouldn't let me. I felt lethargic and lifeless. I got my quilt and snuggled up on the sofa in the lounge. My body felt heavy, and I felt strange. I wasn't ill or anything; it was as if I had a heavy burden on me, but I didn't know why. This happened to me for three days. I just lay on the sofa with no get-up-and-go. Mrs Jarvis saw me lying on the sofa but never said a word to me. What was it with this lady with the big heart? After the three-day lie-down, I was up and running again. I still didn't have the urge or desire to do drugs, and I was a little bit confused. I began to feel different and very strange. It was as if a huge burden had been lifted off my shoulders.

I also recall one day when I bumped into Mrs J as she was coming out of her office. We both said our hellos, and then Mrs J said to me, "God said He wants you to come to church." I said, "I don't do church, and could you please not ask me again, as I definitely will not be going!" After my confusion about God growing up learning a little bit about the Islamic faith back in 2001-2002, church was the last place I wanted to go. Don't get me wrong—I went to weddings, funerals, and christenings, but those were the only times I actually stepped foot in a church. I knew that God existed, as I'd never believed in evolution, and I also believed that on the day of judgement we all would have a chance to explain to God all the wrongs we'd done on earth and He'd understand and forgive some of us, and then it would be off to heaven, where all the forgiven ones would live forever.

Although I wasn't taking drugs anymore, I started to have a drink with some of the residents in the house when Mrs Jarvis left Brooke House and went home. At first it was the odd drink here and there, but then it became a regular thing in my life. I would drink to get drunk. My addictive personality was still at large. This frightened me, as I recalled Mrs Jarvis and a resident named Clarke talking about a Bible passage (Luke 11:24-26). In this passage, Jesus says, "When an unclean spirit goes out of a man, he goes through dry places, seeking rest; and finding none, he says, 'I will return to my house from which I came.' And when he comes, he finds it swept and put in order. Then he goes and takes with him seven other spirits more wicked than himself, and they enter and dwell there; and the last state of that man is worse than the first.'" I recall thinking, "Oh my God! I'm clean from heroin and crack cocaine, and now the drink wants to take over and attack me seven times as much; I had better take this drinking easy!"

As time went on, I still went out almost every day to shoplift and make money from it to buy the nice things in life. Most things I shoplifted, but things like my Ugg boots and my Ugg scarf I paid cash for. I also went and paid for some Adidas Cribs. Those are just a few of the many things I acquired through my grafting. My collection of belongings was getting to a point where I wouldn't need to buy or steal for a very long time. My wardrobe was growing at such a rate that I seriously considered investing in a new wardrobe. I had high-end toiletries, fashion jewellery, perfumes, nightwear, and even optical wear (I paid extra, as I received an NHS voucher because I was claiming benefits). I paid extra for my glasses; I chose a pair of designer frames and had the lenses thinned out. I also invested in disposable contact lenses, which I paid for with cash. In the space of one month, I'd easily made a few thousand pounds including the clothes and all the other things I now owned, and I always had money in my pocket. I recall waking up one morning about a week after coming out of jail and doing my make-up and hair in the mirror. I had to look not once or even twice but three times, because I no longer resembled the old me! I woke up, and over twenty years had left me! Not just my face but my hair also looked different. My hair was full of life, bouncy, and in really good condition. The skin on my face and my body was youthful, and my figure was taking on a new shape. I was using the same soap and body lotion I'd used all my life, so what was going on? I also had a prolapsed womb and was due to go to see my doctor to make an appointment to see a gynaecologist, but that had also disappeared! What was going on? I walked down the road and people stared at me. They were not the stares I'd become used to when I was on drugs; no, these were looks saying, "Who's this woman?" I got lustful stares from men of all ages; women looked at me with admiration, envy, or respect. Admittedly, I loved every stare and glare. Not only did I feel alive, but I looked alive too. Men half my age were hitting on me, and when I told them that I was old enough to be their mother, they told me they didn't believe. Some I'm sure were turned on by it, and some were gutted, as I *was* too old for them. Some knew but refused to let my age get in the way of trying it!

Another time in Brooke House I was in the kitchen making a drink and telling some of the other residents about my prison tactics, and Mrs Jarvis walked into the kitchen whilst I was telling the others how I was clairvoyant and how I'd met a woman in jail who was a spiritualist who had told me about my grandmother who had passed away in April 2002. Mrs Jarvis just looked at me but didn't say a word. I thought nothing of it (well, why should I?) and just continued to tell my stories. I'd heard somewhere that Christians didn't believe in spiritualists, mediums, clairvoyants, and so on. The fact that I never charged anyone for a reading meant I wasn't operating in evil, didn't it? I also never gave bad news to people. Don't get me wrong; I warned them of situations and enemies and things to beware of, but I never revealed a death or a tragedy. I simply told them about their past, present, and future. I always closed each meeting with the Lord's Prayer. However, I did invoke spirits without fully understanding what I was doing. Some spirits seemed calm and friendly, and some seemed evil and angry. I was pinned down by spirits in bed a few times after doing a reading. The force was physical, but I don't see anyone there. The presence was heavy and very uncomfortable. Most of the time this happened, I was unable to talk. The spirit paralysed my mouth as I fought to say the Lord's Prayer. There were also times when I woke up in the middle of the night and there was a strong presence in my bed trying to get sexual with me, and that was so damn annoying! I used to get really vexed, and as soon as the strong hold let go, I'd curse and swear, and it would soon go as my fear switched to anger. But none of that stopped me from practicing clairvoyance. I really didn't understand the powers behind it. However, the Ouija board was something I'd never messed with; it had never appealed to me, and I knew from hearing other people's stories that things could get so serious that the only way to rid of the evil of the spirits invoked by the Ouija board was deliverance from a man or woman of God. No one ever told me about the spirit realm; I knew absolutely nothing. I just found myself telling a fellow inmate back in 1997 her past, present, and future. The only encounters I'd had with spiritualism were visiting a tarot card reader a few times when I worked in the betting shop back in 1992-95 and having a reading done by a clairvoyant just before I went to HMP Brockhill in 1996. However, I couldn't read everyone, as I believe some people have a barrier so you can't get in. The secrets of invoking such spirits were revealed to me by the devil himself, so when I say that I knew absolutely nothing, I mean no man or woman had informed me how to practice sorcery. It was because I had been taught by the devil himself that I was able to intrude on peoples' hidden secrets.

 I recall one day leaving my room in Brooke House and walking toward the living-room. I had to walk past the main office on my way. As I neared the office, Mrs Jarvis was standing outside. I greeted her and then found myself saying that I would come to church on Sunday.

As soon as the words were out, I could have kicked myself. I remember thinking to myself, "What did you say that for, you fool!" But I am a woman of my word who doesn't like to go back on it without a good reason, so church it was on Sunday! This conversation took place early in the week. Later on that week, I received a letter from Mommy (the lady who prayed for me before I left prison). The letter was full of hope and plenty of well-wishing. Also in the letter she told me to read some scriptures from the Bible, but I didn't know how to look for these chapters and verses, so I asked Mrs J to help me to understand. Also living in Brooke House was a guy named Clive, who was a church member and had some knowledge of the Book of Life, so he showed me how to look for chapters and verses. After going through the Bible and reading the verses from the chapters I'd been given by Mommy, I really didn't have a clue what they were on about. There's absolutely nothing wrong with my reading and writing skills, and I have an understanding of life itself, but this Bible I could not understand. Mommy also wrote about ten Psalms for me to read at night before I went to sleep, but the only one I was at all familiar with was Psalm 23. I only knew the first two lines: "The Lord is my shepherd; I shall not want."

Sunday of that week came much quicker than I wished. Fortunately, the service didn't start until 1.30 p.m., so I'd have plenty of time to hit the shops before church. Sunday was my best day for shoplifting by far. Although the main stores and fashion shops didn't open until 11 a.m. on Sunday, it was my most profitable day. So I planned to hit the shops as early as possible, sell the goods, and then return to Brooke House with my cash. Then I'd go to church. Even though I didn't believe in going to church, I wouldn't go to church and then go shoplifting. I believed that was a bad omen. So I got up that morning, and as I was planning what shops to hit and where to go, something came over me. I remember feeling lethargic. I had no energy, no get-up-and-go, no oomph! I really can't explain what exactly came over me that day. All of a sudden, when it was almost noon, I started to feel a bit more energetic. It was far too late to go out grafting now and get back on time for church, so I just put it down to a gut feeling that maybe I shouldn't be going out that particular day. Although I'd said I was attending church, I planned to stay for an hour, and then I was getting out of there!

I arrived at church at 1.30. I had been warned by a couple of the residents that the Pastor, Mrs Jarvis' husband, was very boring. One resident told me that even God Himself fell asleep when the Pastor preached! I can honestly say that it wasn't as bad as I expected, but I wasn't going back in a hurry. So what was said in church that day? Well, the Pastor told us a story about a man who gave his wife a to-do list every day. This wasn't just some ordinary list; it was very important, because if she had ten things to do that day but only managed to do seven or even nine of them, then in his eyes she had failed. I didn't understand the parable and didn't dare to ask, as everyone else in the congregation seemed to understand what the Pastor was saying and I didn't want to appear thick. I kept quiet and left it at that. The Pastor also mentioned how to hear directly from God. Yes, how to hear God's voice! He mentioned the four keys to hearing from God and told us to write them down. I thought to myself, "I don't need to write this down; I'll remember these four keys." Before I got back to Brooke House I had forgotten them. I recall thinking that I could always ask Mrs J if I really wanted to know, as she came to Brooke House every day. What else did I think about church? Well, let me put it this way: I wouldn't be rushing back there in a hurry! The following Sunday came around pretty quick. To this day, I don't know what made me go back to church. All I know is that I'd stopped taking drugs and was now having a drink every night, as there were a few alcoholics in Brooke House. It was quite an eye-opener, really, that I'd started to drink pretty heavy. Don't get me wrong; I've drunk alcohol in the past and quite enjoyed the feeling and the taste of certain spirits. However, never before had I drunk alcohol to get drunk; I had only drunk it to be sociable. Now it was as if I had a time limit and had to get it down my throat quickly. It never occurred to me that a lot of former heroin addicts use another drug or alcohol as a substitute. So why am I telling you this? I believe I went through this experience to show me that I was not at all in control of drugs or alcohol! I truly believe that God used this knowledge to grip me with His mighty hand and lead me to church, because I never wanted to go back. I planned to go shoplifting. I had a stiff neck, but it wouldn't have stopped me from doing what I wanted to do, which was to go out and graft. So there I was in church with a slight pain in my neck and a face on me like a wet weekend in Brighton! The Pastor began to preach the word, and all of a sudden he looked straight into my eyes as if he was speaking to my soul and said something that gripped me with fear! He was talking about what losing your conscience is like. "It's like having a deep cut on your arm. It hurts at first and can be quite painful. But if you keep prodding at that wound, it eventually becomes numb." That's what had happened to me! I recall thinking, "Oh my God! How can this be mended?" He also went back to the to-do list he had spoken about previously. The woman in the story represented human beings. Her husband represented God. The to-do list was the Ten Commandments. So I had to keep all Ten Commandments to do God's will? Well, that was my salvation out of the window! I had broken all ten! But what this man of God was saying was that even if you break only one commandment and diligently carry out the remaining nine, you're not obeying God's Ten Commandments. A lot of people think that as long as you don't murder and have no other gods, then you're safe; that's what I thought too at the time. I thought if you broke one or two, such as by telling a lie, you were not as bad as someone who had broken all ten. What am I trying to say? To do God's will we must obey All Ten Commandments as a package. If we lie, then we are no better than a thief or a murderer. He also went on about the four keys to hearing God's voice. This time I wrote them down so as not to forget. The Pastor also said that we should always ask God if what we had been taught in church that day was true. What freaked me out more than anything on this particular day was the way the pastor looked into my eyes. He knew my name, as he was married to Mrs Jarvis, but she didn't know what I was doing on a daily basis. In fact, he knew nothing about me. I came to the conclusion that the message in church that day was definitely for me. After the service, Mrs Jarvis walked over to the congregation and spoke to each and every one of us. When she greeted me, she asked how I was. Instantly, the drama queen came right up to the surface. I told her that my neck was a little stiff and laid it on so thick that even I felt sorry for me! All of a sudden, she laid her hands on me and began to pray and speak to the spirit that was causing the pain. To my absolute surprise, when she finished praying, she looked straight at me and said, "Jesus said there's nothing wrong with your neck!" She then walked away. I was gobsmacked! There was a slight pain, but she was right. I was overreacting; there was absolutely nothing wrong with my neck, as I'd have gone shoplifting with this little pain and thought nothing of it. She also took no time to confirm that the spirit in me didn't want me to be in the church. If I was perfectly honest, I had to agree.

 Later on that night when I was in my room, I used the four keys to hear from God and asked Him if what was said in church that day was true. After a short while, He said to me, "Yes, most of it was the gospel." I then asked Him, "So how do I get my conscience back?" There was no answer. What I should say is that I didn't wait for the answer. I began to pray with an open heart and earnestly asked the Father to please mend this damaged and broken conscience of mine. I found myself opening my heart and telling Him all my wrongs and pouring all my troubles before Him. The last sentence was something like, "Father, I know you can hear me, so please answer my prayer, Lord, as I've come to you for compassion and forgiveness, amen." I felt as though a great weight was lifted off my shoulders. God never really stood a chance of getting a word in edgewise, as I just laid all my problems at His feet. After I prayed, I didn't wait for a response from God, but I knew deep, deep down that He had heard me and that I was not being ignored.

Clearing my conscience did play on my mind quite a bit. I suppose it was fear, because I knew deep down that you're not supposed to steal and lie to get through life, but these wrongs had taken me over and had become my way of life.

It was a Saturday morning, as I recall, and a mate of mine was out on a community visit from prison. We planned to meet early in the afternoon. I had told her that I'd get her some clothes, so I went shoplifting. I returned with a lot of goods for both of us, but I couldn't find it in me to charge her anything, as she was in prison and was like a daughter to me. We met, and I gave her the clothes. When she left, I decided to go out again, as I wanted some money; I was getting used to having money in my purse to buy what I wanted. I entered a designer shop and took two or three jackets (one was worth £500.00) into the changing room where no one could see me. I began to do my thing, but then my phone started to ring. It startled me, as this shop was situated in the city centre in a shopping mall where I'd always had trouble getting reception on my phone. I looked at my phone to see who was calling. It was Mrs Jarvis. I tried to continue to steal, but I couldn't carry on. I felt bad. I would have earned a tidy sum, but I just couldn't do it, especially with Mrs J on the other end of my phone. I decided to leave the shop empty-handed. Mrs Jarvis had called for a chat. I found myself asking her if she wanted a hand running Brooke House. She said we would talk about it when she was in on Monday, but we spoke after the church service on Sunday instead. We talked for a little while, and she explained that she would allow me to help run the house as a volunteer, which suited me. At last someone who was totally aware of my criminal record was giving me a chance! I started work in the house. I told myself that I needed a few quid to see me through until I got my benefits sorted, so I planned to go out one last time to steal. As I got ready, I planned what shops to go to. Just as I was about to leave, my conscience kicked in, and I recall thinking, "I can't work with people who have recently been released from jail and go shoplifting." I also couldn't do that to Mrs Jarvis. This woman was giving me a chance to get a grip on my life, but what was I going to do for money? I had become accustomed to having money in my purse at all times. I found myself sitting down on my bed and praying to God for help and advice. Now that I'd taken that big step in asking God for help, how was I going to cope financially? I'd admitted that I could not go out and steal anymore because I felt bad, and it was not fear of being caught that was stopping me. Although Mrs J was willing to take a big chance on me, this position was a voluntary job, which meant I would work for nothing, although I would eventually receive benefits. My criminal record was terrible. I had over fifty offences and twenty-nine convictions, and I had lost count of how much time I'd spent behind a steel door looking at prison walls. I had now confessed that I knew what I was doing was wrong, but I had never lived on benefits alone. I had always had to steal, as Job Seekers Allowance was something like £65.00 per week, and I knew I wouldn't get the full amount because of the number of crisis loans I'd had over the years. So how was I going to cope? I was also in a bit of a predicament, as I was waiting for my current application for benefits to be processed. I really wanted to send a couple of the girls whom I'd met on my last jail tour some clothes and money, as I knew what it was like to be in jail and finding it a bit tough. The problems kept on flooding my mind. I knew I'd be tempted to steal, because it was what I did as a way of life, and although I was willing to try to change, I also knew it wasn't going to be easy. A couple of days later, I heard from some of the girls who were still doing their time, and the urge to go out and get them something was too strong. I spoke to God again, and this time I went before Him with justification in my heart to see if He would understand that I was contemplating to steal but for a valid reason. All I wanted was to be able to go and graft a few quid to see myself all right, to get a few things for one of the girls in particular, and to have enough money to be able to post the clothes to my mate. So I got ready to go out, and as I was almost out of the door of my room, I felt something in my heart. Because I'd been on drugs for such a long time, my feelings and emotions were usually totally numb, so when I felt this tug on my heart-strings, it jolted me to face God, because what I was about to do was not right. Even though I could sort of justify my intentions, theft is theft, and "thou shall not steal" is a commandment and not a suggestion. I deflated and sat on the edge of my bed and began saying a silent prayer to God. "What shall I do, Lord? I'm not asking you for money, because although I don't really know you, something inside of me knows that to ask God for money is a very bad omen. What I want to know, Lord, is what do I do? Please help me, Father; please give me the solution to this major problem." I was sat waiting for an answer from God when my door opened and in walked Mrs Jarvis! I recall looking at her and thinking, "Why has she just walked into my room?" but I couldn't say anything, as I was totally gobsmacked. She had never walked into my room without knocking and waiting for a reply, so why had she just walked straight into to my room this day? Before I could say anything, she looked at me and said, "God told me to come and give you this." In her hand was some money. My mouth was open, and I was totally freaked out. I thought it was a set-up! I started scanning the room for CCTV but soon realised that there wasn't any sort of camera's hidden anywhere, and even if there had been, cameras cannot read your mind, and I had prayed silently. I sat in amazement and wonder. I looked at the money and then back up to God and back to the money again, as I couldn't believe what was happening.

A Note from Yvonne Jarvis

It was not my desire to help Amanda in any way. I accepted her into Brooke House as a matter of duty. When I first set eyes on Amanda, I was determined to watch out and was almost certain that she would be out of Brooke House soon. "She will not last one week in the house," I thought. Most of the time, I find myself doing what goes against my own personal opinion. I wanted to be quite aloof with this young lady called Amanda, but I found myself giving her messages from God. I had to give messages to her to find peace in my own soul. I guess you will see some selfishness in that. I don't; I see how we are all connected in God. If I am asked to give Amanda money and I obey, I feel some freedom and peace. Why would I do something that would make me uncomfortable just to prove that I did not like Amanda? In helping others, you are really helping yourself. That is the connectedness.

Chapter Eight

DIVORCING THE DEVIL

AFTER I'D BEEN working at Brooke House for a couple of weeks, I started to change. I wasn't the same woman who had walked through that door. Mrs Jarvis gave me loads of advice on doing my job, and we developed a mother-daughter relationship. She used to call me into her office or the conference room for a chat and to pray for me, and sometimes she would tell me about things that had happened to me in the past and things that were to come in the future. I told her how I'd got into practicing clairvoyance and that it came very natural for me to sit down with people and just start telling them about their lives. Mrs Jarvis, however, told me that what I was doing was dealing with evil spirits which explained why I sometimes got attacked after doing a reading. Whenever she spoke to people concerning their pasts and futures, she always told them what she believed God had told her to say. Basically, she heard from God a lot of the time. One day we were in the conference room talking and she became very spiritual and said to me, "God told me to tell you that you were married to the devil." The words were said with conviction, and because of the life I had led, I knew it was a message from God. She also had mentioned to me a few weeks before that I had to be very careful when speaking to God always to make sure I was in God's presence before I opened my mouth to speak, as the devil wanted me back badly and would creep in whilst I was praying to God, and that was quite scary. I asked her, "How will I know God's presence?" She said, "You'll know," and smiled at me. I knew she was very spiritual because of the things she'd said to me and to others in the house. I never told her the specifics of the drug addiction and drug abuse, my ex-partner, the life I'd led, and so on. She was always spot on, never wavering or trying to guess about my life. Nor did she ask any questions; she told it like it was. She also said to me that she knew I was very spiritual because she had heard me telling the other residents about my tactics with clairvoyance. She went on to tell me that I was not clairvoyant; I was a child of God. A child of God hears directly from God. God speaks to all His children, but He gave me a gift to foresee and to speak His word. I knew that was true, because God had told me to tell Mrs Jarvis something a couple of days before this conversation, and I had delivered the message and watched as God revealed Himself to me and Mrs Jarvis. She also told me that I would not become a drug worker which is what I wanted at the time because of my experience. That was the only thing I believed she had got wrong, as I was on a mission to counsel other users because of the lifestyle I'd led for many years. I knew so much about the lifestyle that I thought I would be able to relate to other people in that situation. It's also a known fact that some of the best drug workers are former addicts. What I didn't realise at the time was that to be a drug worker you have to offer an alternative legal drug to replace the illegal drug, and as I know from experience, the alternative drugs don't work the way God does. I cannot offer drug users a substitute drug. I began to let the phrase "married to the devil" penetrate my mind. All the bad things I'd done in life were swimming around in my head. I'd stolen, lied, dishonoured my parents, committed crimes on the Sabbath rather than serving God, committed adultery, and the list went on and on. Surely if God said I was married to the devil, then I must have been. I began to feel sick with dread that God Himself would have His work cut out with me! I then did what I'd learned to do best and pushed the thought to the back of my mind. That bit of information was too deep to sit and ponder on.

Later that night, I was sitting in the living-room watching TV with Elaine. All of a sudden, my whole body seem to be on fire. I was itching from the crown of my head to the soles of my feet. For the past few months I'd suffered this itching all over my body periodically but had not found out what was causing it. But on this night it went to another level. I felt as though I really was on fire. I'd been to my GP about this itching, and he had prescribed some shower gel and some cream to stop the itching, but I'd not used it as yet, as the problem had subsided. Typical. I was sat scratching like a madwoman, but I didn't want to go to my room and apply the cream. I suppose I thought it would calm down and then I could watch my soaps in peace. Elaine turned to me and said, "Why don't you try out the shower gel you got off your doctor?" She was right. I went to my room, and by the time I got there I felt like screaming; it was getting unbearable. I began to remove my clothes quickly and decided to get in the shower and use the gel. Then, once out of the shower, I'd use the cream to prevent further itching. I put my dressing-gown on and grabbed the shower gel, my towel, flip-flops, etc. I was just about to go to the communal showers when I plonked myself onto my bed and looked up toward God. My itching stopped as quickly as it had started. I clasped my hands together, closed my eyes, and found myself asking God, "What do I need to do to divorce Satan?" I didn't expect to hear what God said to me next; nor did I want to believe that I'd heard it! His voice was cool but firm and brooked no argument. He said, "You know what you have to do." I immediately opened my eyes and looked around my room. At that moment I felt dread and great sorrow. I recall saying, "No, God. Please, no!" He didn't say anything more. He went silent, but I visualized Him sitting on His throne with His arms outstretched as if to say, "You asked, and I answered." I then began to obey the voice of God. As I looked around my room, everything looked different, tainted. I didn't realise it at that time, but God had opened my eyes. The enormity of what I had been told to do sank in, and I couldn't pretend that I didn't know what I had to do. I stood up and walked over to my wardrobe. I opened the doors, and all my worldly belongings seemed to look back at me. I saw all my lovely clothes I had acquired with ill-gotten money or stolen them from the shop. I slowly took my jeans out of the wardrobe and grieved as the realisation hit me. I remember taking my least popular jeans out first, as getting rid of them wouldn't hurt as much. The devil was creeping back in, and I realised that if I held back anything, even so much as a vest top, then there was no point in doing what I knew needed to be done. I shrugged the devil off and began to take all my clothes out of the wardrobe. There were piles of clothes, and there were some that I'd never got a chance to wear that had price tags still on them. I then looked at my Ugg boots and Ugg scarf that I loved so much, but like I said, there was no point in just getting rid of a few things. No, this was a divorce, not a trial separation. After I cleared all my underwear, clothes, pyjamas, coat's, jewellery, trainers, shoes, toiletries, perfumes, hair extensions, and cleaning fluids, I sat on my bed like a little girl waiting for the next instruction from God. He told me to put them in large, see-through bin liners and then He would give me my next instruction. I had a few see-through bin liners in a drawer in my room, so used them to put my things in. I was completely stripped. My make-up was ill-gotten as well, as were all my hair products. It would be fair to say that the only thing in that room that was not ill-gotten was one old dressing-gown that my mom had given me a while back, some flip-flops that I had kept from a jail sentence, a pair of cream-coloured stretch jeans I'd never worn, and a brown floral top. I also had a couple of pairs of knickers that weren't stolen and one or two bras. Once I'd packed everything into the bags—and there were a few bags, I can tell you!—I sat and waited for the next instruction. I believe the Holy Spirit led me to do what I did next. It was still the voice of God, but it came from within, and it was gentle and calm. I did not have any control over the next instruction. It was now past midnight, and everyone had gone to their rooms. I walked as if in a trance to the kitchen and opened the door which led to the back garden and began to place all the bags outside. Not once was I scared and not once did I stop to think of the danger of being outside in the dark alone. As I went to and from my room carrying the bags, I realised that I was still wearing my glasses, which had also been paid for with stolen money, and my mobile phone too. I quickly put my contact lenses into a bag with the solution I used to clean them, my mobile phone, and my glasses. After I took the final bag out of my room and to the garden, I locked the kitchen area and began to walk through the living-room to my room. As I was walking, I heard a load groan. I stopped dead in my tracks and looked over my shoulder. As I went to continue to walk towards my room, I distinctively heard the same deep, gut-wrenching groan again! This time I stood tall, threw my shoulders back, held my head high, and took one final look over my shoulder to let the devil know I had heard him but was not about to entertain him with argument, conversation, or fear. I smiled and carried on back to my room. I couldn't believe what had taken place in a few hours. I called Mrs Jarvis, and because she was the one who walked into my room with the money that day after my prayer to God, I thought she should know what had happened that night. She was shocked when I told her, and she said that she had wondered why God had told her to take me shopping that week-end. She also asked what I was doing with the clothes and offered to take them to a charity shop, but I told her that God had told me to put them in the back garden for the night, and in the morning I was to put them on the street and leave them and walk away. It was a very emotional conversation, and I realised just how much this woman meant to me.

The following morning I woke up and looked out of my bedroom window and saw all my stuff neatly packed up in the back garden. I didn't feel too bad, as it goes. I quickly went into the kitchen, and there I found Johnny, the house security guard and care-taker. I asked him to give me a hand with putting the bags of clothes and other stuff on the road next to Brooke House. I didn't want any of the residents to bring anything from the bags back into the house. As far as I was concerned, this was going to be the last time I ever set eyes on my belongings. I felt I needed to explain what I'd done and why I'd done it to Elaine, as I knew she'd understand and respect why I couldn't give my belongings to my family or friends. The fact that they had all been acquired through criminal activity meant that if I had personally given them to people, then it would not have been a complete separation. I also believed that I would be passing my tainted goods over to them, and that could be seen as passing a curse over to them. I also felt that because they were ill-gotten, I wanted nothing more to do with them. I wasn't about to give them to anyone because of what they stood for. No, I had to tell her that they could not return into this house for specific reasons. It didn't take long for a couple of the other residents to discover that there was a load of new clothes and belongings on the street. When I told them that they had belonged to me and that they must not under any circumstances bring anything from the bags back onto the premises, some of them thought I'd gone completely mad. It wasn't just the residents that thought I'd gone too far with this "God thing." as they all termed it. My mom was very surprised and thought that Mrs Jarvis had put me up to it. I was hurt to think that my mom would think anyone could talk me into doing something so drastic, especially as I'd started to find the real me! The fact that I was no longer in bondage to the devil meant victory for me and the beginning of getting to know who I really was on this earth. The purpose for which I had been created was starting to dawn on me.

After my divorce, I sat in my room having conversations with God morning, noon, and night. God opened the eyes of my understanding and taught me how to read the Bible. Every day when I woke up I asked God, "What am I to do today, Lord?" He spoke to me and instructed me, and sometimes He led me to scriptures in the Bible which told me what I wanted to know. The way God moves is awesome.

Liberation Outreach Ministries International Birmingham is the name of our church. It was founded by Apostle Steven Richards based on a vision he had whilst in the presence of God (2 Corinthians 3:17, Luke 4:18-19). Mrs Jarvis often travelled down to London to the church head-quarters. On one trip, I went with her, as she wanted me to give my testimony. I'd also have the pleasure of meeting Dr Stephen Richards. We sat in the congregation whilst the apostle preached the word of God. He then handed the microphone over to Mrs J, who introduced me, and I stood and gave my testimony. I must stress that before I went up to speak in front of all these strangers to proclaim that I was a drug addict and a thief before Jesus took me out of the lions' den, I was extremely nervous and felt couldn't do it alone. I looked up towards heaven and whispered, "Help me to do this, Lord. I depend on You." Before I knew it, I found Mrs J standing with me in front of many people. I had an unction that made me bold and fearless. The Holy Spirit took over, and I gave my testimony to about fifty strangers. After my speech, the apostle laid his hands on me and prayed. I recall hearing all the congregation praying in tongues, and the next thing I knew I was on the floor. I was shocked. I felt as though I was being pushed, and I tried to fight it. Then I realised that no one had touched me, and no one had pushed me! In the end I gave up. I fell flat on the floor and couldn't get up. I felt strange. Eventually, after around ten minutes, I stood and walked back to my seat.

After I stepped down off the pulpit, I went and sat with the congregation, and there was a finger buffet for everyone. I sat with Mrs J by the entrance to where the food was laid out. Basically, you had to pass Mrs J and me to get to the food. Everyone made their way towards the buffet. Most of the church members greeted me and said that I had given a powerful testimony and shook my hand and said "God bless you", but some of them seemed angry and ignored me. I wasn't bothered in the slightest, but I was annoyed at their ignorance. "Why are these people angry with me?" I thought. "Surely this testimony signifies that the God they serve is a living God; why are they not rejoicing?"

A Note from Yvonne Jarvis

I did not initially pay much attention to Amanda's story even though she told it more than ten times in the presence of others at Brooke House, at meetings, or in the church. Why? I did not trust Amanda. "What is she scheming?" I pondered. We travelled to the parent church in London, and Amanda told her testimony to the women at the Women of Worth

Conference. That was when it hit me that this woman might have been touched by God. I was not going to be excited without cause. Hence, I began to watch Amanda's ways. She was so crude in faith—she had no interest in anything but knowing God. "However Amanda's life goes, she seems ready to embrace it. I'll watch her for twenty-eight days! I'll watch her for three months!" Those were my thoughts at first. Then I started to be reminded that with God, all things are possible. I began to embrace the changes I was noticing in this young lady.

Although the walk has included challenges, Amanda has picked herself up several times, it would seem! Alas! No, it is all being done by God's mercy and grace. Amanda has been sovereignly touched, incapacitated, and prevented from operating by the flesh and has been set free from drug addiction and dishonesty.

Word hit the street, and quite a few people heard that I'd moved on by taking such a big step. Some thought it was a phase I was going through; others admired the fact that I'd truly done some soul-searching. Some were pleased to see that I was no longer committing crime or taking drugs and consequently was no longer being thrown into prison. One of my aunts (my mom's sister) brought me a lot of really nice clothes that she hadn't worn along with some she had worn but had taken good care of. Mrs Jarvis went shopping and bought me a lot of nice jewellery and underwear and tops, and she also put clothes in carrier bags and brought them to Brooke House and told me to have them. She also said if there was anything that was too big or not my style, I was to leave them in the bags and she would collect them back from me. My wardrobe was looking healthy again. I did not miss any of the items I had got rid of. That is a big puzzle to me, I must confess.

Chapter Nine

WHAT DRUGS CAN DO TO A SOUL

I'M NOT GOING to say that any of this was easy, because life isn't easy. All I know is that since I came out of prison, I can honestly say that I have been gripped by the Father's mighty hand. When I was taking drugs and committing crime, I often used to think that God couldn't save me, as I'd done too much wrong in my life. I used to think that God does not forgive us for all our sins. I was also led to believe that God does not forgive us for murder unless it's justified in the eyes of man, in the sense that you can only be forgiven if you can justify murdering someone. That is a lie of the devil. I also recall taking hundreds of pounds worth of class A drugs and not wanting to wake up the next day. I really didn't want to live most days, as my days on this earth consisted of drugs for breakfast, grafting through the day—I suppose I could call that lunch, more drugs for dinner, and then even more drugs for supper. I sit back and think of the places I've visited because the drugs had full control of my life. I walked the streets for hours some nights lonely and cold with nowhere to go. Lots of my drug associates were only too glad to have me stay over at their places, because I used to give them drugs in payment for the privilege of sleeping on their sofas for the night. Sometimes I used to test them by telling them that I didn't have any money or drugs when I asked if it was OK for me to kip on the sofa until the morning. Some of these associates grudgingly let me stay, believing I had nothing except the clothes I was wearing. I suppose they were thinking of the money I would earn the next day. At least they were going to get some drugs then! Some were so blatant that when I asked if I could stay for the night, they made up some cock-and-bull story and made excuses, but when I pulled out my stash of gear, the tune changed in a nanosecond.

I should also share a story about the time I was living in London with Darren. We were waiting to score drugs in a drug user's flat. I sat with Darren as we waited for the dealer. A woman was also there with two of her brothers. She was an enemy of mine, and I couldn't stand the sight of her. She'd only been out of jail a couple of days and was still celebrating her freedom with her brothers. The dealer arrived, and we all scored our drugs. I felt like I was going to pass out and collapse from rattling (another word for detoxing). As I got my foil plate ready for a much-needed smoke, I saw my enemy and her two brothers cooking up their gear and ready to inject. I'd never injected heroin before and had never been drawn to this way of taking heroin. There was also another woman in the flat who was just about to inject the heroin into her groin. I'd never seen anything like it before and felt really sick. All of a sudden, I noticed that the woman whom I regarded as an enemy was lying on the floor and her lips were going blue. To this day I don't know what came over me; it must have been God. I was horrified but very calm as I informed the people in the flat that she had gone over. They all looked at me and then at her body on the dirty floor, and to my shock and horror, they were more interested in having their hit than in helping her! Her two brothers were more interested in getting the needle in their veins than helping their sister, who was at death's door. At this point I was almost throwing up due to an intense rattle. I calmly put my foil down and felt her pulse. She had stopped breathing. Remaining calm, I made a circle with my index finger and thumb and placed it as a barrier on her lips. I then placed my lips on the circle I'd made with my finger and thumb and began to give her the kiss of life. I'd never done this before, but my main concern was to blow life back into this woman's lungs. I did this a few times and proceeded to pump at her heart. I did this for about two or three minutes, but it felt like a lot longer. No one else seemed interested. They were more interested in their fix, her own brothers included. She coughed at long last and came back to life. I thanked God. I was then overcome with love for this woman, and all animosity went out the window. After a while she thanked me, and it came to light that she had paid for the drugs that her brothers and this other woman were too busy with to care about her dying! We became drug mates, and the next day she took me out grafting with her, as she was what's known as a kiter (someone who uses stolen credit cards in shops and stores and forges the signature of the true owner to obtain money and goods by deception). We were supposed to split the money 50-50, but she paid her brother more than me and all he'd done was tag along. I didn't go out with her again after that, but it showed me that in this dark life you either wise up and swim or you drown. After what I'd seen, I became a swimmer of an Olympic standard going for the gold medal. I saved her life whilst her brothers stood by and were more interested in saving what was in a needle, and after all that, she ripped me off! The drugs are that powerful. They controlled everything—the lifestyle, the food you ate or didn't eat, and the thoughts that went through your mind. When I was on drugs, I never liked other drug users even though I was probably more devious than them. It's only now that I have the love of God in my life that I have come to realise that drugs have a powerful spirit behind them. The drug has full control whether the person realises or not. How many times have I heard people say, "I can control my habit"? how many times did I say it and truly believe it? I lost count. Crack cocaine lifted me up so high that I was puffed up with arrogance and pride. I felt like a giant in the drug den. Some people would literally do anything you told them to once you had that powerful powder in your hand. You had the drugs in your right hand and the drug users' dignity in your left. Because I grafted for my own drugs, the praise for my style, even to my own ears, was very embarrassing. People would tell me what they thought I wanted to hear in order to get me to sort them out. In reality, they just belittled themselves before me and my drugs. Personally, I could never beg anyone for drugs; I would give them a lot of patter (manipulating talk), but I wouldn't beg.

I would then take heroin to bring me down, as the high isn't always nice when you've smoked too much crack. What a dangerous place to be day in and day out! No wonder prison was a welcoming place of rest for my soul.

A Note from Yvonne Jarvis

So many things that Amanda has said and written about her dark days are outside my experience. I believe that because of my innocence, Jesus protected me from ever seeing or knowing Amanda during those dark days. I even struggle to believe the stories. I struggle to believe that this woman who is now in my care knows so much about drugs, let alone that she has experienced everything she has spoken or written about. I only believe because I have checked her stories with her mum, Christine Tweed. When she narrates her version, she chokes, cries, and goes into a depressed state just relaying what Amanda has said about all these experiences.

Can you imagine waking up one morning after you have had a strong addiction for almost thirteen years, opening your eyes, and not knowing that you have been delivered from such a powerful thing? I'd tried loads of times to come off drugs. I'd tried with the aid of prescribed drugs and cold turkey. I even thought I could do it by monitoring how much I was taking and cutting down. I failed every time. I called out in the pit of my soul for help, but I thought it was a useless thing, as no one could hear me. I used to tell myself, "One day I'm going to get off the drugs and be a somebody." The truth is I never believed it. The cry for help was inside my head. I would smile on the outside or tell people I was fine, but inside I felt as though I was dead, beyond repair, heading to the pits of hell; and I couldn't wait to get there, because surely it would be better than living this sorry life.

The drugs don't just destroy your soul; they destroy your life. I knew a few people who died because of drugs, and the devastation they left behind no amount of crying could mend. Drugs are evil and are a way to self-destruction. It's not just the person who takes the drug who's affected; his or her family and true friends feel the pressure that living a drug-fuelled life brings. I've often described drug addicts as victims of a very cruel addiction.

I certainly made a lot of mistakes. Once I got caught shoplifting, and because I was rattling and really didn't want to spend a week-end in the local police station, I gave my younger sister's name as my alias. Another time I used the name of my friend Laura. Both women were angry with me. There were times I was sold out to the drugs, and I haven't met a user who never crossed that invisible line. If they never had the bottle to do such things, they certainly thought about it.

Chapter Ten

FINDING JESUS CHRIST

I CAN CONFIDENTLY say that I have it on good authority that there *is* a God. He's a living God, and I now have the privilege of serving and being served by the living God. I feel His presence when I pray to Him, when I worship Him, and when I lay all my worries and cares at His feet. He ministers to me. He puts His arms around me and tells me He will not leave me nor forsake me (Hebrews 13:5). There is nothing too big or too small for Him. He is mighty, merciful, and compassionate, and His name is Jesus. He did so much in my life when I didn't know Him, especially when I believed He was only a prophet of God and no longer alive. I believed miracles only happened when Jesus was physically on earth, and now that He was gone, that was that! How wrong I was. I was also blinded by the works of Satan and didn't have the knowledge that He was there in the beginning when God the Father created heaven and earth (Revelation 1:8 and Genesis 1:26). He is alive today and has always been alive, and

He's still performing miracles by the second. He's an all-knowing God, which means He really does know everything about everything. Forgive me for preaching, but I cannot seem to keep this secret to myself. I also have to boast about God because He not only took the drugs out of my life but swiftly removed the damage they had done to my brain, the damage that surgery could not fix. What am I talking about? It is a fact someone who's been hooked on heroin and crack for such a long time may physically come off the drug, but mentally it is impossible. There has not been a day to date when I have had the urge to smoke. I have no triggers. (A trigger is a situation or image that can cause an addict to experience a craving for a drug. For example, if someone used to use tinfoil to smoke drugs, although they have come off the drug, when they see the foil, it triggers something in the brain, and immediately the drug comes back to the front of the mind.) When I see foil, drugs don't spring to mind. When I see a small glass bottle, a plastic water bottle, an inhaler, or anything I once used as drug paraphernalia, it has absolutely no effect on me. I have been cured of such thoughts. That isn't the only damage I had; no, I was being eaten up inside by worry, hate, stealing, and lying—all the things that people endure whilst living deep in sin. It's no wonder I thought God didn't want to know the likes of me.

 I had a lot of demons destroying my soul. My ears were spiritually covered with sin, and so were my eyes. When I heard people talk about demons, I used to think to myself, "You can't say something like that to someone; demons are monsters!" I used to see *demon* as a very insulting word, but now I know the truth. You need knowledge of the Bible to understand and gain wisdom about life.

 As you have read, I now know the truth. God does forgive, and He certainly loves us all no matter what we've done or haven't done. How do I repay my love to God when I've never loved anyone? To say I never loved is a bit harsh to my ears. I loved my grandparents with a passion, and I love my family. If I truly love my family, how come I couldn't stop the lifestyle I led? I can put my hand on my heart and say I never fell in love with any of the men that were in my life. Lust is the correct word and the correct emotion. Now that I have allowed Jesus to take control of my life, I know what true love is. Love is when you would do anything for someone. I know that I'm not alone when I admit that there is more to love than meets the eye.

I'm at a place where I'm becoming dependent on God for my life. My life is now the life of Christ. Yes, I still make mistakes. I'm still learning how to abide in Christ totally, and I'd be lying if I were to lead you to believe that I'm finding it really easy. It's not, but it's not difficult either. Let me explain. The hard part was learning to let ill feelings go. Submitting to God is a learning curve. What I failed to realise is that God understands every man and woman, every boy and girl, every situation. After all, He created us in His image and likeness, and He created all things (Genesis 1:1-26). Getting my head around what God has done in my life is a big thing, and I can say that I never played a part in it. All the power and the glory belong to God. The easy part of my walk nowadays is the daily worship, praising to God and speaking to Him and listening when He speaks to me. The Holy Spirit helps me to read, understand, and obey the Bible and to go to church and keep God's commandments. Imagine your loved one telling you that he or she loves you, will do right by you, and will do anything for you. Imagine he or she says all these wonderful things to you but doesn't allow you to share your feelings. How would you feel? That would be a lack of communication. That's what it is like if we don't allow God to speak to us. Don't stop praising God and thanking Him for what He has done for you, but allow Him to speak to you too. If you make yourself available to hear the voice of the living God and obey His instructions, abiding in Christ is possible. A continuous practice in this manner is yielding a fruitful result in my life. As the Apostle Paul said, "I die daily" (1 Corinthians 15:31). I have realised that I am dying daily to my own desires. In other words, this is a daily surrender to God by faith. The gifts God gives to us are pure, unadulterated, and unconditional, and yet I still question why He saved a wretch like me.

As I sit and write this true story, I realise that God is my all. My mom and others have said that they believe I have gone from one addiction to another. When I first heard that I was taken aback a bit, but my attitude towards God is devotion, not addiction. The difference is that when I was addicted, I *had* to have my drugs; I *needed* to have my drugs, because I was addicted to them. Although I have to have God and I need to have God, I also *want* to have God. I enjoy having God, and I could not live without God. He has chosen me to do His will. I am honoured to tell people that the creator of heaven and earth desires to have true fellowship with me. He desires to have fellowship with you too if you will allow Him in so that you too have a testimony of what God can do in your life. The Fruit of the Holy Spirit are supernatural. They are love, joy, peace, longsuffering, kindness, gentleness, goodness, faithfulness, and self-control (Galatians 5:22). Jesus Christ is the only way that we may bear such fruit.

In the next chapter, I will talk about how I fell away from God. It is important that I share this with you, as I'm doing God's will and not my own. Let me explain. I turned to my Lord and Master, because life without Christ is a crisis. I made a big mistake in taking God's love for me for granted. The most important thing about falling or stumbling when walking a Christian walk is getting up again. If you fall or stumble a thousand times, get back up a thousand and one times. Repentance is a must if we're to have fellowship with the Lord. The precious blood that Jesus Christ shed on the cross was not in vain. It was shed so that we believers could go to the throne of the most-high God in the name of Jesus Christ and repent with our hearts and ask Him to have mercy on our souls and to forgive us our sins as we forgive others. We can ask Him to show us the right way, the only way. The fact that we are saved by the grace of God is enough for us to recognise the love of our Father in heaven.

A Note from Yvonne Jarvis

I find it so easy to understand what salvation is. I really must share my illustration of salvation with you. Before I do, let me say this: no theologian or man and woman of faith can emphatically disagree with what I will share.

First of all, go to your Bible and do this exercise. Substitute the word life *for* salvation. *Then consider this truth. The only life that does not perish is the life of God. John 3:16 says, "For God so loved the world that He gave His only begotten Son, that whosoever believes in Him should not perish but have eternal life." In John 17:9, the only definition of eternal life is given. Here it is: "And this is eternal life, that they may know You, the only true God and Jesus Christ whom You have sent." It is so exciting to note that these two verses are spoken by Jesus Christ Himself. So the only definition of the eternal life given us is what Jesus gives us and none other. When you substitute* life *for* salvation, *bear in mind that you are saying salvation is eternal Life. Eternal life is knowing the true God and Jesus Christ. Are you still with me?*

How can I know God and Jesus Christ? My flesh cannot know God; I can only know God by God's Spirit, who is the person of the Holy Spirit. Do you remember this? "But God hath revealed them unto us by His Spirit: for the Spirit searcheth all things, yea, the deep things of God" (1 Corinthians 2:10, KJV). Any life that perishes is no life. Therefore, the only life that is and will remain forever with God is eternal life. Salvation, life, and God are equivalent. I've got salvation. I've got life. I've got God.

"If God is for us, who can be against us?" Amanda has salvation. God is for her; that is why no demons or forces of darkness can pull her back into the destructive life she once lived.

Chapter Eleven

THE BIG FALL FROM GOD

I FOUND IT hard to allow God to take full control of my life at first, because I had so many bad habits and was very rooted in my old ways. This is why I say that I die daily; my deliverance didn't happen overnight. When I first realised that God was real because of the miracle He performed in my life, I sort of took it for granted that God loved me so I was free. Yes, I am free from bondage (Galatians 5:1), but that doesn't mean I can now relax and only call on God when I want Him to answer a prayer. Yes, He will always love us, but please don't try to tempt or deceive Him. What am I saying? I'll tell you about the time I fell, and it was a big fall.

After I'd been saved and was living a clean life, I was running Brooke House as a support worker and managing the house by making sure the other residents kept the house rules and so on. Because of my responsibilities as a house leader and support worker, I had to be alert. As some of the other residents were in the same predicament as I had been when I first arrived at the house, I was able to sit down and tell them where I'd been and that there was a future for everyone. I didn't go around Bible-thumping or quoting words from the Bible; I simply told them how God had changed me and my life. It gave a few residents a glimmer of hope when they heard that my criminal record was much bigger than theirs and my drug life had been very bad. I never once hid anything from anyone, as I didn't feel I needed to. As time went by, I had dealings with the West Midlands and Staffordshire Probation Service, police officers, and service user charities (ARCNO support team and Stanhom Housing). The reason I had dealings with those organizations was that I was a support worker. I counselled some of the residents who I felt needed counselling, and I also supported them by making sure they didn't miss their appointments, and on a few occasions I had to go along with a client to the doctor, dentist, or even shopping if they were incapable. All in all, I enjoyed my job, as it was something constructive, and I felt that I was putting something back into the community. Dealings with the police were an everyday occurrence, as they came to Brooke House to monitor one of the residents who was on a curfew and had to be there from 7 p.m. to 7 a.m. Sometimes they turned up three times in one night to make sure this person was in the house or because they wanted to catch him out; either way, they were doing what police do. As house leader, I answered the door when anyone called, and I introduced myself as the leader. I always told the residents it was up to them how to handle being on police bail, probation, or curfew. As long as they didn't expect me to lie for them or cover up for them, I would give them all the support they needed. Some residents didn't like the fact that I was no longer criminal-minded, some didn't believe that I no longer thought like a criminal, and some really didn't understand. When I had any spare time on my hands, I went to my room and spent it reading the Bible, praying, and building up a relationship with Jesus. As I'd got rid of my glasses, I sometimes asked God when I would get my eyesight back, but as I believed by faith that He would restore what I'd lost, I wasn't stressing over it.

Five weeks after I got rid of all my ill-gotten belongings, I had a slight headache from trying to read the Bible, as it was irritating my eyes. I had the money to go to the optician and buy some disposable contact lenses, but something drew me to begin to pray and ask God to give me my eyesight back. I remember placing my hands on my forehead and pleading with Him. I believe I was led by the Holy Spirit, as peace came over me all of a sudden. After I prayed, I felt complete peace and somehow knew that God was working on my eyesight. I was going to make my way into the city centre to meet my mom and also to purchase my lenses. Brooke House is a non-smoking environment, so if you want to smoke, you have to go into the back yard. I decided to go out into the yard for a fag before leaving the house to meet my mom. As I walked out into the yard, one of the other residents was smoking. As I lit my cigarette, he said to me, "I've got something to tell you, but I don't want you to say anything to Mrs J." I asked him what was it so secret that he didn't want Mrs J to know. He told me he had found my glasses on the branch of a tree on the side road by Brooke House. I almost choked on my cigarette as I digested this piece of information. He pointed to a huge tree right next to the back yard. I didn't say much to him; I left the house after smoking and went to meet my mom. I called Mrs J and told her what had happened that morning. She was praising God and told me she would be over to the house later, as she was out with her grandchildren shopping. When I saw my mom, I told her what had happened that morning, and she was puzzled. I don't think she believed that my prayer had been answered; she thought this was a coincidence. As a result of getting my glasses back, I gave the money I was going to use to purchase the lenses to my mom, as she was broke.

I returned to Brooke House a few hours later to find Mrs Jarvis sitting with a couple of the residents. Amos, the man who had said he'd found my specs in a tree, was also present. Mrs J asked him to go and get my glasses out of his room. When he brought the case containing my specs down to us in the living-room area, my heart skipped a beat, as I instantly recognised the case. Mrs Jarvis opened the case, and there were my glasses, exactly as I had left them. Mrs J and I asked Amos to be totally honest and tell us where he had got the glasses, how long he claimed to have had them, and why he had decided to admit to having them in his possession. He said he had seen the glasses case in the tree about four days before. He then took them off the branch and took them to his room, as he wanted to give them to one of his daughters, but when he saw me trying to read books and paperwork, he couldn't do it and so decided to let me know that he had them in his room. I believed him simply because it had been five weeks since I'd thrown my stuff out with the glasses, and if he'd taken them out of the bag then, he'd have given them back to me a week after I got rid of them, as I recalled that he was one of the residents who did not agree with me throwing my optical wear away. Even my mom and Mrs J thought I'd gone too far with getting rid of those lenses and the glasses. Mrs J took the case and went into the spirit realm. When she opened her eyes, she confirmed that Amos was telling the truth and that my glasses had been placed on the branch by an angel. However, the angel was from the forces of darkness; this wasn't an angelic angel. She said not to worry and that we needed to destroy the glasses, because Jesus had told her that if I had placed the glasses on my eyes without seeking the Lord through prayer, then I would have been back on drugs before the end of that night. I believed her, as the taste of crack cocaine had returned to my mouth for a split second in the morning, but I had just disregarded it. Also, the day before, I had had a big argument with Elaine about the correct way to smoke crack cocaine. I found myself defending the drug and getting quite angry with her, as I was a master at crack and felt that she was trying to tell me otherwise. Mrs J stood in the midst of this commotion but didn't open her mouth to say a word to me or Elaine. However, she did tell me that she thought I should go and apologise to Elaine after the argument. I went to Elaine's room and said I was sorry, and I recall thinking to myself, "What was all of that about?" I also couldn't understand why I had felt the need to defend a drug which was no longer in my life. I also found it a bit weird that I had resisted the urge to take the glasses from Amos when he told me that he had them in his room. Mrs J said a prayer over the glasses and sanctified them with the blood of Jesus Christ. After she did that, I was able to put the glasses on, and my eyesight was restored. I know I serve a living God, and the living God serves me.

    I carried on as normal doing my job. I'd had a few dealings with the police, the probation service, charity service users, and the prison service regarding referrals. Whenever any of the authorities called, they asked to speak to me. I also had information regarding any referrals faxed to me regularly. As this was a rehabilitation project for people with problems, the aim was to rehabilitate the homeless, people who had been released from prison, alcoholics, drug users, and people who had difficulty learning life skills. After all, it was ARCNO that had referred me to Brooke House via the prison service. Whenever I received any previous conviction papers, I immediately handed them over to Mrs Jarvis, as I didn't want to know about the residents' personal dealings with the government. I really wasn't interested, and I knew when I was in the same situation as the residents, I didn't appreciate people who didn't work for the authorities reading about my criminal past and my drug misuse. Apart from that, Mrs Jarvis had clearly said to me that all such information was to be passed on to her. Not once did any of the authorities that used Brooke House as a service provider check who I was; they just accepted me at face value based on my telephone manner. I believe to this day that that was the work of God. My life had drastically turned around, and everyone I came into contact with saw honesty and had no reason to believe I would be untrustworthy. I am not criticizing or laughing at the service users; I'm pointing out that God Himself was moving mightily in my life. I also believe that most, if not all, police officers have a strong discerning spirit and are able to detect when people are not being truthful. I had nothing to hide and was perfectly honest to each and every person to whom I spoke. He is the Holy Spirit who is working within me doing the work.

One of the service users referred a man who had recently been released from prison. His name was Mark. We started dating and ended up having a relationship. We slept together a couple of times, and I clearly recall not being able to pray to God after the first time we'd slept together, although it did feel right sleeping with him at the time. I told Mrs Jarvis that I was in a relationship with Mark, and she was not happy with the situation. She told me that it was not God's will for me to be with someone in the dark. She told me to go and seek God. I feel I have to stress that she didn't judge me or make me feel like I had sinned. What she did do was guide me back to God. I went before the Lord and prayed. I recall saying to God, "I'm not sorry for what I have done, because I haven't done anything wrong, but there is a reason why I couldn't pray to you, so forgive me, Father, and show me the error of my ways. Show me my secret faults." I also didn't believe that the God I served was going to be discriminating, so I began to plead my case about the relationship I was in. Little did I realise that I had an idol in my eye when I took Mark to God in prayer. I truly didn't know what to say sorry for. I hadn't committed adultery, and my knowledge of God was very limited at that time. I now know that it's a serious thing to be saved and then to disobey God in such a careless way. God rebuked me by taking me out a couple of days after I sinned. Let me take you on this awesome journey. I was getting ready to worship, and I felt the grip of God on my person; His presence was very strong. I immediately sat on my bed and waited for Him to speak. The Holy Spirit told me to shower quickly and get dressed. He even told me what to wear. I did what I was instructed. When I was dressed, I was fiddling about in my room, and the stern voice of God came to me, telling me to drop what I was doing and leave my room. It catapulted me out of the door. I was trembling and trying to move as fast as I could. I went out of the front door and onto the road, and He directed my steps by telling me to turn left or right. By now I knew that God was taking me to Brooke Vale Park, which was about a ten-minute walk from Brooke House. I was directed to go a different way. If I walked too quickly, the gentle voice said, "Slow down, child." When I got to the park, the most eye-opening, amazing thing happened to me and my surroundings. The Holy Spirit led me around the lake where there were ducks and swans. As I looked at my surroundings, God showed me things in great detail. The water that normally looked dirty was clean, clear, and beautiful. Although I do think that the ducks and swans are lovely creatures, they looked absolutely beautiful, and they had God's glory upon them. As I walked along the path, God pointed out little things that I had never noticed before. Although the path was primarily for pedestrians, vehicles did use the path at a 5 m.p.h. speed limit. I heard a car behind me, and as I was about to look back, God spoke, telling me not to look back. I looked back, thinking that it was my inner voice. I was told again, "Do not look back," and the voice was stern, unlike the first time I heard it. I spoke to God and said, "I looked back because I heard a car behind me and didn't want to get run over by it." He answered me by telling me to trust in Him and not to look back but to have faith in Him and keep on walking and listening to His voice. As I continued to walk, God showed me two men and a dog. I asked Him, "Why are you showing me this, Lord?" He replied, "The man with the dog is selling the other man drugs." When I looked properly, I could see myself scoring off a dealer. I could also see myself selling drugs to a punter! God then spoke again and said, "So now that you can see what I wanted you to see, do you want to go back to that life?" I shook my head and said, "No, God, I do not." He didn't reply to that. He told me to keep walking, so I did. As I got to the other side of the park, everything I looked at had God's glory and was beautiful. Even the rubbish was pretty; the weeds looked like beautiful flowers on a glorious day. The dust on the ground was not dirty; the houses opposite the park were immaculate in appearance. I was then led towards a man on a park bench with a couple of bags on the ground, and his head was buried in his hands. God said to me, "Take a good look." Although it was a man on the bench, I immediately saw myself when I was on drugs, homeless, and stealing to fund my drug habits. I felt so sad for this stranger that I recall wanting to put my arms around him and tell him everything would be all right, but God wouldn't allow me to. As I walked away and blinked, everything looked ugly and tainted, the way I'd seen the park in the past. The glory of God was snatched from my sight in a split second. Although I knew that God was still with me, His presence eased up, and I instantly knew that God was showing me that without Him, I was nothing. I discovered later on that day that the power of God is powerful. It sobered me up somewhat as the realisation began to sink that I could easily have been like the people I had seen in the park if not for God's anointing. I returned home after my walk, and I was beginning to know the fear of the Lord.

Whilst in prayer to God, I asked Him to show me a sign regarding Mark. What I still didn't realise was that I was going to God with Mark in my thoughts. I was willing God's words to me to be ones I wanted to hear. I also said to God, "Every time I have prayed to You, Lord, You have shown me something really nice about him." I was going before the Lord with an idol in my eye, and the God I serve and the God who serves me gives His children their heart's desire. God even showed me in dreams what Mark was really like, but I truly believed it was Satan trying to play tricks on me. I'd seen that Mark was not a nice person and was full of lies and deceit. A stranger told me in my dreams that he was a two-timer and wasn't really interested in me but thought I looked good on his arm to impress his cronies. I continued to have a relationship with Mark, as I believed that I was doing nothing wrong and that God had shown me the nice things about Mark. After we slept together again, I started praying to God with my mouth and not with my heart. When God clearly spoke to me that day, His words were very clear: "I command you not to sleep with him again!" I was mortified! I began to argue with God, saying, "How can you say that to me, God? I'm in a relationship with him; it feels right. He is my heart's desire, and what could possibly happen if I sleep with him again?" God didn't answer me. A vision flashed before my eyes that I couldn't ignore. I saw myself lying on my bed with a lot of blood between my legs. I wanted to believe that it was a trick of the devil again. I also wanted to believe that it wasn't God's voice that I had heard; deep down in the pit of my tummy, I knew it was the voice of God.

For the next three weeks we continued dating, but every time we were alone, Mark grew tired and fell asleep. I knew this was the work of God, because when He told me not to sleep with Mark again, I told God that the relationship between Mark and me was intense and that as we'd already slept together it was likely to happen again. I also said to God in prayer that if He commanded that I not sleep with Mark again, then God would have to do the work for me, as I believed that we were doing the most natural thing on earth as man and woman. My period was late that month, so I took a pregnancy test and discovered I was pregnant. Mark and I sat and talked about it, and I decided I was keeping my child with or without him. So that was it—I was having a baby! I was so sure that God's commandment was only for a while, as I was bringing a new-born baby into the world. When I say I thought it was only for a while, I mean that I truly thought that the commandment only stood for a few weeks. Now that I was officially having a baby, God would forgive me if I slept with Mark again, because I was now pregnant and sleeping with him wasn't going to alter the fact that I was now an expectant mother. We slept with each other Thursday night, the day after I did the test, as I believed the damage or deed had been done. In the past, it had felt normal and natural, but on this night I came face-to-face with the devil of old. Mark spoke and acted in exactly the same way as my ex-partner Darren, and my eyes were finally opened. God had shown me signs in my dreams that this man was not what I wanted him to be, and I had ignored the dreams even as I knew in my heart that he was all the things that God had shown me. After that night of lust, that final time, I surrendered and asked God to show me the man I believed to be the one for me, and I asked God not to hold back to spare me any humiliation. God didn't hesitate in showing me what sort of person Mark really was. It is my prayer that God the Father has mercy on Mark's soul. I also pray that God has mercy on my soul, as I didn't take heed and disobeyed the voice of God.

It was a Saturday morning when I woke up and saw the pool of blood between my legs. I was shocked even though God had shown me what would happen if I slept with Mark again. I hurt so much and couldn't bear the fact that my disobedience had cost me a life!

A couple of weeks after the miscarriage, I left Brooke House, as I didn't want to be in the house with bad memories. I no longer worked there, I'd split-up with Mark, and I'd lost my baby. I'd lost my job, as ARCNO had been informed by another resident (who was a mate of Mark's) about our relationship. It wasn't only the relationship that lost me the job. One of the ARCNO employees had given Mrs Jarvis the impression that she was disgusted that Mrs Jarvis could have an ex-offender with a string of convictions longer than most clients she had dealt with working in a place where other ex-cons resided. Mrs Jarvis had made it quite clear to me that Alice didn't like the fact that I had moved on with my life and the credit was not going to ARCNO, as they were the support team who had referred me. I wasn't too bothered by what was said; however, it seems that when you move on with your life in a positive way, certain people don't accept the drastic change. That statement is not a fact; however, it is my personal opinion, and I am entitled to voice my opinion. I felt cheated. The world owed me too much. I was hurting inside, and I wanted to continue to hurt, as it seemed normal to hurt after what had happened during those few weeks. God wouldn't allow me to carry such hurt. He showed up and showed off yet again in my life and snatched all the hurt and pain from me. I returned to my parents' home in Stechford. Although I still prayed and worshipped God and was still hearing from God and still poured my heart out to Him, something was missing from my life. I initially thought that once I was no longer in Brooke House, it was going to be hard to keep this relationship with God, but I repented before the Lord and was a lot more diligent in seeking Him. I was alone in my room a lot of the time. The fact that I repented helped. I was also led by faith to fast for twenty-one days, which I believe made me weak so that God could reveal Himself to be strong in me. The Holy Spirit continued to minister to me, comfort me, provide for me, and wrap His spiritual arms around me, and His angels had complete charge over me. I did slip a couple of times by having a bottle of wine here and there. I could drink two or three glasses of wine or sherry, but then I found that I couldn't look up to God to pray earnestly. The grace of God was upon me, and I quickly remembered that I was now a child of God. I had to pick myself up and repent every time I did wrong in the sight of the Lord. I felt God's presence come down on me, and His presence was so acute He couldn't be ignored.

A Note from Yvonne Jarvis

"Rejoice not against me, oh mine enemy: when I fall, I shall rise; when I sit in darkness, the Lord shall be a light unto me" (Micah 7:8). This was the passage I kept meditating on when Amanda went out of the place of safety I believe God had prepared for her. I asked God a lot of questions and got no answers. I fell ill and could not eat or drink. I was confused and disillusioned; I coughed blood and struggled to breathe. I was in bed for seven days. All through this period, when I prayed, all that came to me was the scripture quoted above. God strengthened me and I returned to work. I wondered what was going on. It was my dark season. Then God spoke to me. I was to pray for Amanda and to forgive. Most of all, I was to revive the work in Brooke House, as all activities were shutting down. We were getting no referrals from the probation service or from ARCNO or the other agencies. I was led to make a decision to convert the service to a bed and breakfast, but I decided to take my time before making any move.

I woke up one morning and heard in my spirit that the house would be full that day. That was what happened. I got up, and at the breakfast table my mobile phone rang. I was to provide accommodation to two people. Then another call said there would be three more. I got dressed and left for Birmingham to keep the appointments with the agencies that were referring these five people. That was the revival of the Brooke House project, and I began to heal from the pains and losses. The most amazing thing was that I kept wondering how Amanda was faring. I had a few panic attacks thinking Amanda had probably gone back to drugs when I got a letter to inform me that she was no longer on the benefit which she had claimed whilst at Brooke House. Amanda had said in one of her testimonies at church that whilst on drugs she never claimed benefit, because shoplifting paid for her lifestyle. I really thought she was back on drugs and the rest of it. I was expecting to be informed that Amanda was back in jail or dead. I could not bear the thought, so I just cast all my cares concerning these thoughts upon Jesus (1Peter 5:7).

Four weeks after I had fully recovered from the illness and had finally got over Amanda, she called out of the blue. "Hello, Mrs J. It's Amanda. How are you?" the voice on the telephone said softly. Wow! I was so surprised to hear that familiar voice, and it was steady, clean, and clear. "Oh, she's back in prison!" I thought. "Amanda, where are you? Are you back on drugs? Have you been arrested or what? Talk to me! I say talk to me!" I yelled. Amanda gently replied, "No, Mrs J. I am fine, and I am living with my mum." "Please tell me the truth, because I know you are no longer on benefits. Have you got a job? How are you supporting yourself?" The questions I asked were almost endless. Amanda replied, "Can I come and see you so we can talk?" We agreed on a date and time, and I really was pleased that Amanda was going to a church, but I was disappointed that she was not happy in the church she attended. I asked Amanda to come back to our fellowship. She seemed pleasantly surprised that she could return to our fellowship. I remember telling her that the church belonged to God, and everyone, including her, was free to attend even if she no longer lived at Brooke House. Amanda came to church, and the story changed for the better from then on.

Chapter Twelve

REUNITED WITH JESUS CHRIST

I WENT TO a Methodist Church with my mom so that I could receive the word from God, but all I received was a banging headache. Please don't get me wrong; the minister was a lovely lady and extremely welcoming, as was the huge congregation. There were black people, white people, old people, young people—all types of different people, but the service itself was very empty. If anything, I came out of the church and was in a horrible mood, a mood I hadn't felt for a long time. I had to take this one to God. He told me to contact Mrs Jarvis, but I tried to protest, as I felt that I didn't want to run to her with every problem I had when it came to learning to walk a life with Christ. In the end, I surrendered to Him and obeyed His command. I am glad that I obeyed Him, because when I called her, it was as if we had never been apart. She asked how I was doing, and I told her about the church I attended with my mom, and she immediately said to me, "Why don't you come back?" I didn't hesitate and was back in LOMI

Birmingham that Sunday. The congregation of LOMI was less than a quarter as large as the congregation at my mom's church, but the word was strong, and I left full of spiritual food. I came out of church with such a spring in my step that I'm sure I bounced all the way back home!

What I would like to stress is that Christianity is not a religion. Christianity is simply having a relationship with Jesus Christ through the Holy Spirit. The relationship is granted to us believers by the grace of God the Father. When you have a true relationship with God, you will have to ask yourself how on earth you managed to live without this knowledge and understanding, without knowing and understanding the love of the only true God. I'm not saying that a Christian way of life is easy to begin with, because it isn't, but to wake up every morning with a solid promise that the Father will not leave me or forsake me (Hebrews 13:5) and that I am forgiven of my sins through the blood of Jesus Christ (Mark 2:10; Revelation 1:5), lets me smile when I rise and worship in the morning.

As I was still living at my parents' home, I wanted my own independence. I contacted the housing department and was told that I had points to bid for a home, as I had been on the waiting list since February 2011. I was getting quite frustrated with the wait and the way that society treated me because I had a criminal record, so I ran to God and asked Him what was happening with my accommodation. Because I needed to know, I sought Him diligently, as I wanted to be where God told me to be. When He spoke and said that I would be moving back to Erdington, I have to admit that it wasn't the answer I wanted. I felt as though I was moving backwards in life. I tried to fight it and gave God lots of excuses and promises that if I could stay at my mom's I would still worship Him and still attend church. I have come to realise that sometimes when we're trying to please God and ourselves, we can get it very wrong. Trusting in God is a must if we're to please Him. When God has a plan for you, He will find a way. After all, He is the author and finisher of our faith. I can now see through the grace of God that moving back to Brooke House was the work of God. After God told me to move back to Erdington, I asked Him to show me a sign why I should move back to Brooke House. Some of my family members openly attacked me, saying that I was taking this Christianity too far, and there was a time when my mom questioned me regarding the Bible, but this wasn't enough for me to want to get up and leave. I was at LOMI church when a Pastor was preaching. He looked at me and clearly said; , "When we are given a word from God and are not sure we often ask God to give us a sign. He read Mark 16:17; "And these signs will follow these who believe . . ." He then concluded his message with "signs will follow us, not us following signs". "I sought God again about moving just to be sure that it was God I had heard from, because the devil speaks to us too, and I really wanted to be sure that it was God who had spoken to me. The spirit in me moved me, and I instantly knew it was God; however, for selfish reasons, I didn't like the fact that I was to move back to Brooke House, but I was not about to disobey God again. You may ask, "How do you know it was God and not your human inner voice? How can you be certain?" The answer is that I can tell by how I feel when I'm about to do something after seeking God. If I feel discomfort, then it's not of God. If I feel peace and boldness, it's of God. You cannot ignore the feeling of peace if you seek God with diligence. I also speak in tongues a lot, and that helps build up my spirit and enables me to keep in line with God. It also enables me to receive from God, as it subjects my soul to the workings of the Holy Spirit. I am now back here at Brooke House, and one of the reasons is to write this book. Although I started to put pen to paper in August this year whilst living at Mom's, it has been much easier for me to sit down and do this here. There were far too many distractions when I lived at my mom's, and I am a person who needs to be focused on what I'm doing, as I've been easily distracted in the past. It is also a fact that the presence of God in this house cannot be ignored. Being back here has been a wake-up call, as I forgot a lot of the things I have been through. It's strange not to think of drugs and to forget sometimes that I actually lived that life. I believe another reason I was bought back here was to face up to some of the demons I carried with me for such a long time before I was reconciled with the Lord. What am I saying? There have been many times in Brooke House when I have seen some old traits that I once had before I found Christ. Since being back here, some of the residents have tried to sabotage the working of God in this home. I recognise these traits immediately as spiritual bondage. Some people cannot handle some of the mind-blowing changes that have taken place in their lives and in other people's lives. They feel a need to destroy any good thing, as they believe otherwise someone else will take it away. In the process, they destroy themselves. Being in prison and living on the streets has a long-term effect on some people, and because of the presence of God moving mightily in Brooke House, some feel that they need to be babysat and will destroy things in the house to get some sort of attention from others. It is because I too have experienced that bondage that God enables me to recognise the behaviour, and it is nothing prayers will not solve. God's hand is very powerful.

Whilst I was living at my mom's, I saw a lot of things that opened my eyes. For the first few weeks, God protected me from seeing drug users and dealers. I walked down the road without seeing a single soul who was from my past life. I walked past phone boxes where there was almost always someone scoring or waiting for a dealer, but I did not see that at all. I believed by faith that God would guide me places. Then one day I saw three drug dealers in the space of ten minutes. One dealer, who was dealing to a couple of users, didn't recognise me at first. He didn't know what to say to me. I could tell that he was embarrassed for selling drugs to me in the past, and I felt great sorrow for him even though he said that he didn't believe it was the hand of God that worked in my life. He couldn't understand that I was telling him that the work he saw in me was not of my doing. It was God who delivered me. I knew my words were falling on deaf ears, but I didn't give up on proclaiming the work of God in my life. After speaking to the dealer, I said my good-byes and began walking down the road towards my aunt's house. I heard a car pull up beside me, and there were two other drug dealers looking at me with puzzled expressions on their faces. One dealer said, "I'd heard that you were around, but I didn't believe that you were clean." Now that he had seen me with his own eyes, he was very subdued. Again I proclaimed the word of God and told him that I really never had a say in what God had planned for me, and to my surprise, he was in total agreement. He too looked ashamed that he had sold me drugs in the past. The biggest shock came a couple of weeks later when I saw a dealer who was called Mr Big. He was big in body and in reputation. He didn't recognise me until he heard my voice. We were standing in a corner shop waiting by the till to pay for our goods. He almost collapsed in the shop! He kept on justifying himself to me by saying that he had never really wanted to sell me drugs and that he had always known I was better than other smokers. I recall thinking, "That's a lie; I was no better than my drug pals. If anything, I was worse, and you know it!" He kept saying that I had a guardian angel, and I noticed that whenever he said this, he looked above my head and around my body as if he could see something. This didn't unnerve me; quite the opposite. He couldn't understand how someone could wake up one day and have the past thirteen years removed. I kind of know where he was coming from, because it took me a while to realise just what God had done in my life. So when I came back to Brooke House and saw the lost souls of some of the residents, the Holy Spirit had His way and moved to a point I cannot explain. God has a way of using me to listen to others who are caught up in drugs and alcohol, and there and then, at that moment when I am with the person and feeling what they are feeling, that instantly puts fire in my belly to get up and do something. I haven't forgotten where I came from. I have all the knowledge of living in the dark, but I feel as though I am talking about somebody who I once knew very well who is now dead.

Since coming back to Brooke House and returning to the church, I have been baptised in water; I was baptised with the Holy Spirit in March and in water in July. I have received the gifts of speaking in tongues, the interpretation of tongues, prophecy, discerning of the spirits, and many more gifts that God has blessed me with, distributing them to me as He wills (1 Corinthians 12:4-11). Some of my family members were a little bit sceptical; they believed it was too soon, because I'd only been a Christian for a few months. Because of the life I had before finding Christ, I needed to be sure that I knew what I was doing. I achieved that by reading the Bible stories about baptism and learning why people were baptised. You have to believe with your heart that our Lord and saviour Jesus died for the remission of our sins and that He truly loves us sinners. He loves us, but hates sin, and He came to the earth that we may have and enjoy life and have it till it overflows (John 10:10). He preaches the gospel and turns us to repentance (Luke 15:7). Once we truly believe that Jesus Christ is Lord and that we are completely free because of what He did for us on the cross, there is no reason for us believers to delay in walking with Him, Jesus our personal Saviour. I still pinch myself at how far my walk with Christ has come. I always thought that being a Christian was a boring way of life: no sex, drugs, partying, or real life. My life is far from boring. I'm free and finally happy. If you asked me if I would give up my walk with Christ for a big mansion, lots of money, holidays, comfort, and all the other desires I had before I was saved, I would confidently say no. I've had a lot of things in life, a lot of money, and a lot of heart-ache. No amount of worldly possessions could turn me away from the God I serve and the God who serves me. I'm not saying that you're not going to go through hard times once you're saved, because that would be a lie; it is known as going through the wilderness. That is where we believers truly experience the hand of God in our lives. What I am saying is that life without Christ is a crisis. Walking in the light is not just about attending church and reading the Bible; it's about getting to know Jesus and abiding in Him (John15:1-12). Now I have truly seen the light, and I walk in the light. I know that no matter what anyone thinks of me, no matter what judgements are made about me and my life (because I know I will be judged), no matter what is put in my path as I walk through life, I finally have reached my resting place on this earth. If God is for me, who can be against me? I have a solid promise from the God I serve: "I will make your paths straight" (Hebrews 12:13). I rest in the comfort of God, Jesus Christ of Nazareth. Amen.

A Note from Yvonne Jarvis

I am humbled by God in Amanda's life. When I obeyed God to answer his calling to start the Brooke House Rehabilitation Project, I only obeyed because I had become restless and felt empty even though I was making a lot of money. There was still a huge void. My life had no joy even though everything good was happening for me. I felt in my spirit that I must respond to the audible voice of God. "My children are out there. They are hungry; go and feed them." The next day, I was out on the streets feeding the homeless. Six weeks later, I was instructed to put a roof over the heads of the marginalised people in the city. I found a sub-standard building owned by a money-grabbing ex-client who promised to bring the house to a good standard but reneged. The project survived a lot of setbacks, and finally we are settled in a beautiful, well-built building. Had I known that I would be faced with so many problems, I probably would have chosen to remain where I was, running my lucrative accountancy practice. Thanks be to the spirit of victory that visited me and now lives permanently in me. Amanda is a product of God's purpose for the calling.

The Diamonds of the Community

As the project proceeded, I was wakened from a deep sleep one night by a loud noise. I thought that there had been an explosion in the house. I ran to my daughter Victoria's room and fell on the floor, totally disorientated. I thought I was having a heart attack and would die. I began to cry out to God in the name of Jesus. Eventually, calm came over me, and I fell asleep on the floor. I heard another bang. It was not as loud as the first one but loud enough to wake me up. I looked up, and Victoria's bedroom door swung open. Right at the entrance was a huge black rock. It began to roll towards me as I was still lying on the floor. I thought the rock would crush me, but I was unable to move. I was just staring at this ugly black rock as it gathered momentum and rolled towards me. Suddenly, I saw a man (whom I knew was the prophet Elijah from the Bible) pick up the rock with one hand and hand it to an immaculate presence. As Elijah handed it to this glorious being who I could not see, though I perceived his presence, I heard the presence say gently to me, "These people you are helping are the diamonds of the community. They come as rough and dirty as coal, but with you and Me, they are refined and become like this." Suddenly, the black rock became pure diamond, and it was handed over to me. As I held the amazingly magnificent rock the size of a football in my hand, *a tingling went over me, and I became joyful. I still have that joy in me today. The immaculate presence then told me, "Remember always that I will never leave you nor forsake you, and I am with you always even until the end of the ages." Immediately, I recognised the person speaking to me was Jesus. I jumped up with joy and started dancing and worshipping. Suddenly, I found myself back in my bedroom in my bed, worshipping aloud in my sleep. My husband, who was by me, joined me in worship, and this continued for a long time.*

I then realised I'd just had a lucid dream. That was the beginning of the Brooke House Project.

A Final Word

A CHANGE OF LIFESTYLE IS VERY NECESSARY

I'M A SINGLE parent to my twenty-one-year-old son. I've lost a lot of years with my boy, but I'm not going to dwell on what has happened in the past, as it brings me nothing but unwanted heart-ache. I don't mean to sound like I don't have a heart or dwell on the sorrows I endured, but things like hearing my son's voice break, parents' evenings, school plays, and just being a proper mom were snatched from us both because I was married to the devil himself.

Now, in order to move on, I am casting all my cares, pains, and burdens upon Jesus Christ (1 Peter 5:7; NKJV). I have learned from the teachings of God and through having a relationship with my personal saviour that when we beat ourselves up and worry about what we should have done or shouldn't have done, it profits us absolutely nothing. We walk with a burden of sin when we do not realise what Jesus Christ did for us on the cross. We are washed of our sins by the blood of Jesus. (1John 1:7). Nowadays, I look forward to the future, as I feel it's a very bright one indeed. I also didn't realise that daily surrender to Christ could bring such a blessed assurance. I become docile as a lamb before the throne of God and take daily instruction, as I am nothing without Him. I also recognise that God is moving mightily in my life, and it's only through seeking Him diligently and obeying His word that one can bear the fruit of the Holy Spirit, namely love, joy, peace, longsuffering, kindness, goodness, faithfulness, gentleness, and self control (Galaitians 5:22-23 NKJV).

Tribute to My Parents

I got away with so much when I was younger because I had an angelic smile that fooled people. I still have that smile, but now it is not to fool people. When I do smile, it is genuine, as it is Christ who is in me that people now see. I was a bit of a daddy's girl, as I was his first child. I so love that man. Having that special bond with my dad makes me realise that I am blessed, because I can easily relate to the Father in heaven and the love He has for His children. People who were abused as children may not know that special feeling of depending on a father or mother whom they can rely on and so may find it very difficult to reach out to God Almighty. That is why I am blessed to know what it is like to have a father's love. I believe that if you do not know what it is like to be loved by a parent, God will touch you in a way that will compensate for the loss you have endured. I also know what my dad felt as he saw his little girl go down a very dark and destructive road, and I know that God feels the pain a hundred times more, because He created us and we are His children. Not only did God feel the pain for me when I was lost, but He also felt the pain for my dad too. God Himself revealed to me through the Holy Spirit that He is a God of reconciliation. Whatever pain we may endure in our lives He removes and puts peace and love in our beings.

My mom is a woman who feels it's a must to worry about her children, like a lot of good moms I know. I keep telling her not to worry, as it brings her nothing but stress. But I feel that's how our mom shows how much she cares for her brood, God bless her. It is my daily prayer that the Lord will appear to my mother as He appears to many of us. My mum's worrying didn't stop me from leading a destructive life or cure me, so what does worrying help? The Lord told me that worrying profits us nothing (Luke12:22-28)

This Is for My Family

Losing contact with my family was due to the prison life I chose to live. I'm not saying that I directly went out of my way to go to jail, but I cannot ignore the fact that I was a criminal twenty-four hours a day, and going to jail was part of the lifestyle. Having a close relationship with my family is very important to me, as I've lost so many years. We certainly put the devil to shame earlier this year at my dad's birthday party in August, when for the first time in over thirteen years, all my mom's children were in the same house at the same time having a good time! Praise God.

To Friends and Acquaintances

I shared with you my journey of my true life and the way I lived. I have learned to forgive and forget the wrongs that people have done to me over the years, as that was the only way for me to be able to have fellowship with my Lord and personal saviour. I've also been an enemy to people over the years, and for your sake, I hope you find it in your hearts to forgive me and forget what I have done to you. You're carrying a burden, and what I did to hurt you is really not worth any sleepless nights. I obtain mercy for my soul because I have mercy on others; I really do! (Matthew 5:7) Have I forgiven the man whom I lived a life of hell with? Of course I have. To be 100 per cent honest with you, if I saw him today and he was thirsty, I'd gladly give him water and probably stroke his head whilst he drank (Matthew 5:43-47). All the things that I endured whilst I lived in total darkness were put upon me by Satan, that devil of old. Although I didn't know it at the time, disobedience to God Almighty often releases curses, and I was disobedient, so consequently I was cursed. I believe through God's wisdom, knowledge, and understanding that I also had a lot of generational curses from my forefathers. I also know and believe that I am a miracle, because what happened to me was a miraculous recovery as I was delivered from evil by the hand of the Almighty God. If you can get to that place where you can look at your worst enemy and recognise that it's the sin that you hate and not the person and ask God to help you to forgive and forget, then, my beloved brothers and sisters, you're half-way there. My prayer for all who read this true story is that the God of our Lord Jesus Christ blesses you with perfect peace in Jesus' name. Amen.

To Readers of This Book

I want you to know that it was hard to recount the dreadful times of my journey, but it's not about me; it's about doing God's will. When I say it was hard, I stress that having to recall all the years when I felt alone and was empty because I didn't know God were painful, because I chose to hold on to the bad memories. The Lord appeared to me and told me to surrender fully to Him and allow Him to move through me to write this book. The Lord allowed me to surrender, and because of His grace and mercy I was able to do so. He removed the pain of my past and replaced it with His peace and joy. It was only after I surrendered to God that the precious Holy Spirit was able to work through me. Consequently I was led by the Holy Spirit to write this book, and its sole purpose is to reach out to the lost souls out there and to let real people know that no matter what they may have done or not done in life, no matter where they may have been or not been, no matter what they're up against, there is a permanent solution that will repair, relieve, and restore them. I was termed the scum of the earth for being a victim of a cruel addiction. I was regarded as the scum of the earth for trying to survive under the pressure of being held in spiritual bondage. People judged me. I also judged me. I used to think that I was unable to be saved, unworthy of the deep love of our Lord and Master that He wants to lavish upon His sheep. That is such a big fat lie of the devil! The Lord wants you to come to Him with all your cares and cast them at His feet while He tells you not to worry. We are worthy because Christ died for us (Hebrews 1:1-4). I must stress that when you call out to God the Father in the name of Jesus Christ with all your heart, you will get an immediate response, as He is a living God. So I urge you to pick up your cross and follow the Lord, our personal saviour, Jesus Christ. Amen.

A Note from Yvonne Jarvis

Are you in doubt that God will help you? Are you in doubt that all those torments you are going through can be brought to a final end in your life? Are you in doubt that your son or daughter can be released permanently from drugs or alcohol addiction? Are you in doubt that your husband or wife can turn over a new leaf? Can your marriage be saved? Can your story change for the better? Are you in doubt that you can change your character or personality? Are you in doubt that you can be made strong? Are you in doubt because of guilt that God will forgive you? Are you in doubt because you feel unworthy of God's help? Are you in doubt that God really exists?

Listen to me, and please pay attention! In his sermon "Doubt: What should I do with my doubts?" Timothy Keller writes, "Doubt is a problem that all of us will face before we come to grips with faith. To deal with our doubts, recognise that they are based on faith assumptions; examine the object of your faith and whether it is trustworthy; and let Jesus' love for you become your reason to have hope."

This is one of the topics that often cause obstacles to belief in Christianity. You may be wondering, "How can I believe for my own specific situation?" "How do I know that the Bible is true?" All these questions have one thing in common. They all share the hallway of doubt. This is going through the hallway of doubt. How do you deal with doubt? How do you overcome it? If you're a Christian, you live a continual life of scepticism or doubt. Storms of life come; you begin to lose faith or hope.

To deal with doubt in all situations, you need to unmask your doubt, examine and understand your faith, and fuel your hope.

Unmask Your Doubt

Examine what you've read in this book. Do you believe that all in the book is true, or are you sceptical? What part do you believe, and what part don't you believe? Why do you believe one part and not the other? Now unmask your doubt; that is, find out what is beneath your doubt. The doubt you have is really a belief. It is an assumption; it is a leap of faith. You can't prove it, but you believe it. You're building your life on the assumption that it is true. Every doubt is faith versus faith, belief versus *belief. It is not faith versus reason. It is not natural versus supernatural. So don't just take your doubts at face value; unmask them. Understand that your doubt is an alternative belief. Some may say, "And so what? Are you being philosophical?" No. It is important to unmask your doubt which leads to the next point: that you need to examine and understand what is underneath the mask.*

Examine and Understand Your Faith

What you don't know might hurt you. You may be making assumptions that might, in the long run, hurt you. If you are reading this book, it is most likely that a lot of your assumptions have hurt you or your loved ones. Your faith is not just an abstract thing. It is not just a so-what kind of thing; it is the compass of your soul. It matters deeply what your faith is. Faith is about trust, trusting yourself into something or someone else. It doesn't matter how strong or how weak your faith is. What matters is what you put your faith in. Who or what are you putting your trust in? Amanda put her trust in Jesus, and she was delivered from thirteen years of drugs addiction. Did you seek help from programmes that promised but did not deliver? How many rehabs have you been to? Maybe you have put your hope in the wrong thing. Like Amanda, let Jesus do the work.

Fuel Your Hope

If you want to fuel your hope, you've got to believe that Jesus is the only way to find rest for your soul and the only lasting solution to your life problems. Receive God's own life in you. Get to know the only true God and Jesus Christ. In John 17:3, Jesus declared, "And this is eternal life: [it means] to know [to perceive, recognise, become acquainted with, and understand] You, the only true and real God and [likewise] to know Him, Jesus [as the] Christ [the Anointed One, the Messiah], Whom You have sent."

If you want to know how, please feel free to contact us. Our e-mail address is MTD@rocketmail.com.

God bless you.

Printed in Great Britain
by Amazon.co.uk, Ltd.,
Marston Gate.